University of

Framework
RE

Anne Keast
John Keast

1

Hodder Murray
A MEMBER OF THE HODDER HEADLINE GROUP

The Publishers would like to thank the following for permission to reproduce copyright material:

Photo credits p.15 *RC Church* CIRCA Photo Library/John Fryer, *Stoup* CIRCA Photo Library/John Fryer, *Altar* CIRCA Photo Library/John Smith, *Font* CIRCA Photo Library/John Fryer, *Pulpit* CIRCA Photo Library/John Fryer, *Lectern* CIRCA Photo Library/John Smith, *Statue of Virgin Mary* © Owen Franken/CORBIS, *Station of the Cross* CIRCA Photo Library/John Fryer; **p.23** *1* World Religions Photo Library, *2* Royalty-Free disc, *3* © Nik Wheeler/CORBIS, *4* © Royalty-Free/CORBIS, *5* CIRCA Photo Library/Barrie Searle, *6* © Catherine Karnow/CORBIS, *7* Royalty free disc; **p.26** *1* © Pat O'Hara/CORBIS, *3* © Lindsay Hebberd/CORBIS; **p.27** *4* © Penny Tweedie/CORBIS, *5* © David Lees/CORBIS, *6* © Pierre Colombel/CORBIS, *7* © Roy Morsch/CORBIS; **p.31** © Bryan Allen/CORBIS; **p.36** © Reuters/Corbis; **p.44** *King* © Flip Schulke/CORBIS, *Churchill* © Bettmann/CORBIS, *Elizabeth I* © Arte & Immagini srl/CORBIS, *Mother Teresa* © Reuters/Corbis; **p.45** World Religions Photo Library; **p.46** *River Indus* © Galen Rowell/CORBIS, *Lumbini* © Alison Wright/CORBIS, *Bodh Gaya* © Roman Soumar/CORBIS, *Golden Temple* © Blaine Harrington III/CORBIS; **p.49** *Zoroastrian* © Tim Page/CORBIS, *Jain* © Lindsay Hebberd/CORBIS, *Baha'i* http://news.bahai.org/ by permission of the Baha'i World News Service; **p.51** *Logo of British Humanist Association* by permission of the British Humanist Association, *Logo of National Secular Society* by permission of the National Secular Society, *Logo of Rationalist Press Association* by permission of the Rationalist Press Association; **p.52** *Darwin* © Stapleton Collection/CORBIS, *Russell* © Bettmann/CORBIS, *Bradlaugh* Northamptonshire County Council Libraries; **p.54** © Reuters/CORBIS; **p.56** © Bettmann/CORBIS; **p.57** Rajinder Singh Panesar and the Interfaith Education Centre; **p.58** *Logo for Inter Faith Network* by permission of the Inter Faith Network, *Three Faiths Forum Logo* by permission of the Three Faiths Forum, *Assisi* © Reuters/CORBIS, *Remembrance service* © Hulton-Deutsch Collection/CORBIS; **p.59** *Charles Clarke* and *National Framework for RE* John Keast, *Meeting at the Inter Faith Network* Harriet Crabtree and the Inter Faith Network, *Young SACRE members* Rajinder Singh Panesar and the Interfaith Education Centre; **p.62** © Richard T. Nowitz/CORBIS; **p.64** *Abraham* akg-images/Orsi Battaglini, *Moses* © Stapleton Collection/CORBIS; **p.65** *Karl Schmidt-Rottluff 'Head of Christ' 1919* © DACS 2005 photo by akg-images/Erich Lessing, *Icon of Jesus* akg-images/Rabatti – Domingie, *'The Light of the World' by Hunt* akg-images; **p.66** akg-images/CDA/Guillemot; **p.67** *The Healing of the Lame in the Temple, illustration for 'The Life of Christ', c.1886-94 by Tissot (1836-1902)* © Brooklyn Museum of Art, New York, USA; **p.68** World Religions Photo Library; **p.69** *Qur'an* © Bojan Brecelj/CORBIS, *Mount Hira* Peter Sanders; **p.73** *Sanskrit* World Religions Photo Library, *Ramakrishna* © CORBIS; **p.75** © Leonard de Selva/CORBIS; **p.77** *Both* World Religions Photo Library; **p.78** World Religions Photo Library; **p.86** *Bar Mitzvah* © Dave Bartruff/CORBIS, *Baptism* © ATTAR MAHER/CORBIS SYGMA, *Muslim man and baby* World Religions Photo Library, *Hindu man* © David Samuel Robbins/CORBIS, *Buddhist meditating* © Chris Lisle/CORBIS, *Sikhs worshipping* World Religions Photo Library; **p.89** *Islam* © Chris Lisle/CORBIS, *Judaism* © Richard T. Nowitz/CORBIS, *Christianity* © Arte & Immagini srl/CORBIS, *Buddhism* © Alen MacWeeney/CORBIS, *Sikhism* World Religions Photo Library, *Hinduism* © Ted Streshinsky/CORBIS; **p.91** © Bob Krist/CORBIS; **p.94** © Royalty-Free/CORBIS; **p.97** *All* John Keast; **p.109** *Temple* Royalty free disc, *St Paul's Cathedral* © Richard T. Nowitz/CORBIS, *Rama and Sita story* © Angelo Hornak/CORBIS; **p.111** © Wolfgang Kaehler/CORBIS; **p.112** *Gandhi* © Bettmann/CORBIS, *Moses* © Stapleton Collection/CORBIS, *Buddha* © Leonard de Selva/CORBIS, *Jesus* akg-images, *Guru Nanak* World Religions Photo Library, *Bradlaugh* Northamptonshire County Council Libraries, *Mother Teresa* © Reuters/Corbis; **p.114** John Keast; **p.117** PA Photos.

Acknowledgements Blackwell (*A World Religions Reader*, ed Markham); CEM (*Teaching RE: Sikhism 5–11*, ed Wilkinson); Heinemann (Ruqaiyyah Waris Maqsood, *Examining Religions: Islam*); Hodder (scripture quotations taken from the HOLY BIBLE, NEW INTERNATIONAL VERSION. Copyright © 1973, 1978, 1984 by International Bible Society. Used by permission of Hodder & Stoughton Publishers, A member of the Hodder Headline Group. All rights reserved. "NIV" is a registered trademark of International Bible Society. UK trademark number 1448790.); Macmillan (*Sacred Texts of the World: A Universal Anthology*, ed Smart & Hecht); Microsoft, Encarta, MSN and Windows are either registered trademarks of Microsoft Corporation in the United States and/or other countries; Penguin (quotes from the Qur'an taken from *The Koran*, trans Dawood); Sri Ramakrishna (Ramakrisha quote from www.ramakrishna.org/uk).

Every effort has been made to trace all copyright holders, but if any have been inadvertently overlooked the Publishers will be pleased to make the necessary arrangements at the first opportunity.

Although every effort has been made to ensure that website addresses are correct at time of going to press, Hodder Murray cannot be held responsible for the content of any website mentioned in this book. It is sometimes possible to find a relocated web page by typing in the address of the home page for a website in the URL window of your browser.

Papers used in this book are natural, renewable and recyclable products. They are made from wood grown in sustainable forests. The logging and manufacturing processes conform to the environmental regulations of the country of origin.

Orders: please contact Bookpoint Ltd, 130 Milton Park, Abingdon, Oxon OX14 4SB. Telephone: (44) 01235 827720. Fax: (44) 01235 400454. Lines are open from 9.00–5.00, Monday to Saturday, with a 24-hour message answering service. Visit our website at www.hoddereducation.co.uk.

© Anne Keast and John Keast 2005
First published in 2005 by
Hodder Murray, a member of the Hodder Headline Group
338 Euston Road
London NW1 3BH

Impression number   10 9 8 7 6 5 4 3 2

Year   2010 2009 2008 2007

Cover photo: Photograph of hands by John Lund/Corbis
Typeset in 11pt Formata Light by Black Dog Design
Internal illustrations by Daedalus Studios (cartoons) and Barking Dog Art
Printed in Italy

A catalogue record for this title is available from the British Library

ISBN-10: 0 340 90408 9

ISBN-13: 978 0340 90408 4

Contents

UNIT 1: WHAT IS RELIGION?

You will find out in ...

Lesson 1: What is religion all about?

◎ Match titles to pictures and statements to develop an awareness of the seven different aspects of religion.

◎ Work out a definition for the word 'religion'.

◎ Understand that religion helps people to answer some really important questions about life and to express your own ideas about some of these questions.

Lesson 2: How can you tell if someone is religious?

◎ Express your own ideas about how you can tell if someone is religious.

◎ Analyse some outward signs of being religious and decide how trustworthy you think they are.

◎ Apply some of the ideas from this lesson, about how you can tell if someone is religious, to yourself.

Lesson 3: Where do you see religion in the world around us?

◎ Identify various places where religion can be found using pictures and captions.

◎ Discuss whether religion can still be important in your life even if you are not religious.

◎ Investigate the link between religion and the place names around us.

◎ Think about where you come across religion in your own life.

Lesson 4: Where can you see religion around here?

◎ Find out how to discover information about religion in your local area.

◎ Choose and present appropriate information for a community website.

◎ Think about how you will feel when visiting an unfamiliar place of worship.

◎ Create a code of conduct for a class visit.

Lesson 5: What is religion actually like in a particular place?

◎ Interpret the symbols that can be found inside a church.

◎ Explain the importance of the main features inside a church.

◎ Link aspects of church worship to the use of the five senses.

◎ Express your own ideas about the type of worship you would prefer.

Lesson 6: So what have you learned about religion?

◎ Find out about the similarities and differences between religious people in their worship and beliefs.

◎ Present your findings as a poster, assembly spot, radio or TV programme or magazine article.

◎ Work with others to complete your task.

◎ Consider whether it is the similarities or the differences that are more important.

1. What is religion all about?

SKILLS

- **matching** aspects of religion to pictures and statements,
- **discussing** and **expressing** your opinion,
- **defining** religion,
- **thinking about** some of the really important questions in life

Hi! I'm Zoe and here I'm showing you some of the aspects about my life.

b) belief

My belief is the sun will come out.

These aspects of Zoe's life are also what we call characteristics of religion. These are what religion is about. You will discover examples of how religious people come across these different aspects throughout this book.

ACTIVITY ONE ....

Match each picture to one of the words below. Then, use the word in a speech bubble that you could write for each picture to show what Zoe might be telling you. An example has been done for you.

a) stories b) belief c) right and wrong
d) community e) buildings f) **ritual** g) feelings

ⓘ What does the word religion mean?

Now you know what religion is about, what about the actual word 'religion'? How could you define it?

To give you a clue, think about what happens when you bend your arm, and what job the *ligaments* are doing. Try to describe what you think ligaments do.

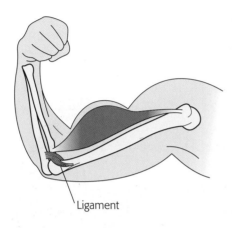

Ligament

Limbs contain ligaments that join or link the bones and muscles together.

ACTIVITY TWO ●●●●●●●●●●●●●

Now look at the letters in re<u>lig</u>ion and <u>lig</u>ament. Can you see any connection? Try to describe religion using some of the same words you used to describe ligament. Use the words below to help you finish this sentence.

Religion means _ _ _ _ _ _ _ _ _ _ _ _ _ _ _ _ _

together   linking   people

ⓘ What can religion be used for?

Sometimes people use religion to help them work out the answers to really important questions about life, like these:

- Why is there a universe?
- Is there any point to being alive?
- What happens when we die?

These are what we call **ultimate questions**.

ACTIVITY THREE ●●●●●●●●●●●

Think of one or two ultimate questions of your own and discuss them in class. How easy do you think they are to answer? Would people agree on the answers? Talk about why this is.

NOW TRY THIS ●●●●●●●●●●●

Choose one of your ultimate questions. Explain what you think the answer to the question is and why.

KEY WORDS

Ritual a ceremony or pattern of actions used in religious worship

Ultimate questions important questions concerning what we believe about life

2. How can you tell if someone is religious?

SKILLS

- **expressing** your own ideas about how you can tell if someone is religious,
- **analysing** signs of being religious and deciding how trustworthy they are,
- **applying** some of the ideas from this lesson to yourself

Look carefully at the pictures of David on the following pages. Each picture is an example of one of many ways that you can tell if someone is religious. Seven of the ways you can tell have been identified in the information section on this page.

ACTIVITY ONE ••••••••••••

1. Complete the caption for each picture to explain how it shows that David is religious. For example, for picture 5, the caption is 'David is joining in the prayers at the school assembly'. This is an example of ritual.

2. Write the word next to each of your captions to show which of the seven ways of identifying religion it represents. For example, David is joining in prayers at the school assembly – PRAYERS.

3. Some of the pictures of David show that he belongs to a particular religion. Use the information and the key words to help you decide which pictures tell you that David belongs to the Jewish religion. Explain the reasons for your choice.

ⓘ Ways of identifying religious people

They might:

- take part in religious worship and ceremonies in religious *buildings*, such as churches, **mosques**, **synagogues** and **gurdwaras**

- say *prayers* or meditate in their own homes

- wear jewellery or special *clothes*, for example, the **hijab** or the **kippah**

- keep special *rules* about how they behave, such as the Ten Commandments for Jews or the Five Precepts for Buddhists

- spend time studying their religion, especially *holy books* such as the **Torah**, the Bible, the Qur'an, the Bhagavad Gita or Guru Granth Sahib

- keep special *rules* about what they eat. For example, Muslims eat only permitted (halal) food and Jews eat only permitted kosher food

- hold special *beliefs* about the world that they are keen to share. For example, Jews, Christians and Muslims believe in one God who created the universe.

KEY WORDS

Gurdwara	the Sikh place of worship
Hijab	modest dress worn by many Muslim women to cover their hair and bodies
Kippah	a head covering worn by Jewish men and boys, sometimes or all the time
Mosque	the Muslim place of worship
Oxfam	a charity that serves the poor throughout the world by helping developing countries
Synagogue	the Jewish place of worship
Torah	the Jewish holy book

David goes to a _____ with his family

David wearing a _____

David _____ with his friend Sol whose pet dog has just died

David going shopping for his mother at a _____ butcher's

David is joining in the prayers at the school assembly

David _____ _____ to Mrs Taylor who is collecting for **Oxfam**

David arguing with Zoe in an RE lesson about something in the _____

Although all of these pictures show David in a religious situation, it is possible that he might not be very religious! People can *appear* to be religious in different ways, but sometimes these appearances may be misleading. Religion is not just about outward behaviour.

ACTIVITY THREE

1. Think about your own life. Make a list of any signs that might lead others to think that you or a friend or a family member are religious. For example, wearing jewellery which is a symbol that is connected to a religion, or visiting a religious place.

2. Do the things that you have listed show that you or the people you are describing are religious or not religious, or are you not sure? Try to explain your answer.

ACTIVITY TWO

For each picture, work with a partner to write a sentence explaining why David might not actually be very religious. The first sentence has been done for you as an example.

1. David did not really want to go to the synagogue, but his parents insisted that he went with them.

NOW TRY THIS

Many people might show some of the outward signs of being religious that you have discussed, but you might have decided that, for various reasons, they are not 'truly' religious. Write a paragraph to explain what you consider to be the characteristics of a 'truly religious' person.

3. Where do you see religion in the world around us?

SKILLS

- identifying where religion can be found using pictures and captions,
- discussing whether religion can still be important in the lives of non-religious people,
- investigating the link between religion and place names,
- thinking about where you see religion around you

Abdul is a Muslim boy who comes across religion every day in different situations and places, like David in Lesson 2. Some of the places and situations are different from those where David finds religion, but some could be the same for both David and Abdul even though they are from different religions.

ACTIVITY ONE ....

1. Look carefully at pictures 1–7 and make a list of how and where Abdul comes across religion.

2. Write down the examples in your list that non-religious people or people from other religions, like David, would still come across.

ACTIVITY TWO ....

Look at your answers to Activity One, question two and discuss the following question. Do you think religion can still be important in the lives of people who are not religious?

1

My family is Muslim and it is one of the duties of a Muslim to pray (salat) five times every day. Often we pray together at home. Sometimes the men and boys pray separately from the women and girls. Sometimes we wear a prayer cap.

I am learning Arabic at the **mosque** school on Saturday mornings so that I can read the Qur'an, the Muslim holy book, for myself.

2

3

Sometimes I go with my father to the mosque for prayers. There is a place for us to wash (wudu) before praying and we leave our shoes outside the prayer hall.

4

Celebrating **Id ul Fitr** is really enjoyable. It is a lovely time, because we give each other cards and presents.

5

We usually watch the news at six o'clock. It is sad that people often seem to be fighting one another over religion in places like the Middle East.

6

Tonight's history homework is about how Henry VIII set up the Church of England, so we don't only learn about religion at school in RE and assemblies.

7

We went on an Art trip to the National Gallery today to look at some sixteenth-century paintings. Lots of them had religious themes.

Where do *you* see religion? You might not find it in all the same places as Abdul.

ACTIVITY THREE ....

Use the heading 'Where do I see religion' and draw a large signpost pointing in at least three directions. Label the directions to show where you come across religion in your life. Draw more than one signpost if you have more ways!

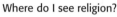
Where do I see religion?

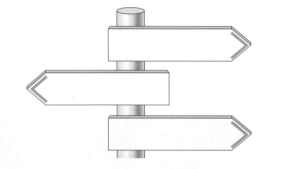

NOW TRY THIS ....

If people are seriously interested in finding out more about religion and experiencing it for themselves, how do you think they would find out about it?

Religion is all around us in the world! Some of the places where religion can be found are special buildings where followers can gather to worship, such as mosques, **churches**, synagogues, **temples** and **mandirs**. But religion can be found in other places too. Many of the names of streets, villages and towns around you have religious connections.

ACTIVITY FOUR ....

1. In small groups look at a map of Britain. Write down all the place names you can spot which have religious links.

2. What does this tell you about the history of Britain?

KEY WORDS

Church	a place of worship for Christians. Other places might include a chapel or cathedral
Id ul Fitr	Muslim festival marking the end of Ramadan, the month of fasting
Mandir	a place of worship and community activity in Hinduism
Mosque	Muslim place of worship
Temple	a place of worship for Buddhists, although the word is also used for other religious buildings

4. Where can you see religion around here?

SKILLS

- **finding out** how to discover information about religion in your local area,
- **selecting and presenting** useful information for a community website,
- **thinking about** your own feelings on visiting an unfamiliar place of worship,
- **creating** a code of conduct for a class visit

You have discovered a variety of places where religion can be found. It can be found at school, in books, in newspapers, on the radio and on the television wherever you live in Britain, but where can you find religion in your area? The special buildings where you can find religion near you will vary from neighbourhood to neighbourhood. For example, there are many synagogues in London, but none in Cornwall! Look at the pictures of Sita and her family here and on the next page, who are Hindu, and see what happened when they moved house.

1

Sita and her family packing up their belongings

2

Sita's family set up a shrine in their new home

3

Sita and her family explore their new neighbourhood and find a mosque and a church

Back at home a leaflet comes through the letterbox advertising the local Baptist church

They go in search of the nearest mandir so they can worship there

Sita and her family eventually find a mandir in a nearby street

ACTIVITY ONE ·················

Write down all the ways and places you can think of that could have helped Sita's family find the mandir.

Here are some clues to get you started.

NOW TRY THIS ············

Look at a street map of your local area. Write down the place names that link with religion. What does this tell you about your local area?

ACTIVITY TWO ••••••••••••

A new community website is being set up and you have been asked to write a paragraph that could be put on it to help new families like Sita's find information about their local places of worship.

Before you start writing you need to plan it! Consider the following:

- Where they can find information about local places of worship (look back to Activity One!).

- What this information will tell them, for example, names and addresses, times of worship, type of services, other occasions like festivals, who leads the worship, and **denominations**, e.g. Jews might want to know if the synagogue follows **Reform** or **Orthodox Judaism**.

As well as the type of information, you also need to think carefully about the best way to present the information. For instance, is it better to use bullet points or just plain text? (Think about websites you have visited recently and how they got their message across to you.)

The following websites might give you some ideas:

www.mkweb.co.uk
(click on religion)

www.lancasterukonline.net
(click on local groups and clubs)

When you have considered this, write your paragraph. Include information about where a new family could get further details, and set the information out clearly – using the websites above as guides if you wish.

However, the best way to find out about a place of worship is to visit it!

ACTIVITY THREE ••••••••••

Think about the last time you visited a place of worship, or if you haven't visited one, what you think the visit would be like. Below are some words that might describe how you would feel as you prepare to visit a place of worship that might not be familiar to you.

a) enthusiastic b) excited c) interested
d) uninterested e) reluctant f) scared

1. Choose the word(s) that you think best describe how you would feel and explain why. Also explain why some words would not apply to you.

2. Are there other words you can think of to describe how you might feel?

3. Places of worship are very special to the worshippers, so you would be expected to show respect on your visit and behave well. Create a code of conduct that your class could use during the visit, to show how members should behave.

NOW TRY THIS ••••••••••

What do you think someone can gain from visiting a local place of worship? Think carefully about this question and write down your ideas. Explain your answer as fully as you can.

KEY WORDS

Denomination	the tradition or teachings followed in a place of worship
Orthodox Judaism	a form of Judaism believing in the traditional teachings of the religion
Reform Judaism	a form of Judaism believing that all the old laws of Judaism do not have to be followed exactly

5. What is religion actually like in a particular place?

SKILLS

- **interpreting** the symbols inside a religious building,
- **explaining** the meaning of the main features inside a religious building,
- **linking** worship to the use of the five senses,
- **expressing** your views on the type of worship you might prefer

We have looked at what religion is about, but what is it actually like in one particular place of worship?

Maria's family are Christians who attend worship at their local **Roman Catholic** Church. There are many important symbolic features outside and inside the building that give clues about the beliefs and practices of those who worship there. Discuss the symbols you can see in these pictures.

Maria and her family cross themselves with holy water as they enter the church

Maria's dad reading from the lectern. This is a traditional lectern

Maria receiving bread during Mass

Maria arrives at a Roman Catholic Church for **Mass**

ⓘ The main features of a Roman Catholic Church

➤ The *altar* is where bread and wine are shared in memory of Jesus' sacrifice on the cross. This takes place in the service called the Mass.

➤ The *tower* or *spire* points people to God.

Crosses and *crucifixes* represent the suffering, death and resurrection of Jesus.

Incense, a sweet-smelling substance burnt to create smoke, is used to represent purity and the prayers of the people rising to God.

The **Reconciliation** *Room* is a place where people can chat to the priest about the things they have done wrong and ask for God's forgiveness.

➤ *Statues* of the **Virgin Mary** and saints are examples of faith that Christians should try to follow.

➤ The *pulpit* is used to give talks. These are usually called sermons.

➤ The *lectern* is for reading from the Bible. This is a modern lectern.

➤ The *font* contains holy water for baptising new Christians.

➤ The *stoup* contains water used by worshippers to make the sign of the cross on entering the church.

➤ The *Stations of the Cross* is a series of fourteen pictures hung around the church showing the events as Jesus was taken to be crucified.

15

ACTIVITY ONE ·················

The previous page shows you the main features of a Roman Catholic Church. Your task is to design a factsheet to help a class of 8-year-olds understand about the features of the church. The information on the factsheet must include:

a) An outline of a Roman Catholic Church.

b) Your own drawing of an altar. Include these objects on it: a cross or **crucifix**, two candlesticks with candles, a **chalice** for the wine and a **paten** with small round wafers on it for the bread. Label the objects in your drawing.

c) Labels pointing to two more features inside the church. You must describe what each feature looks like and what their significance is.

d) The reason why the altar is the focal point in the church.

e) A short description about how you would experience each of the five senses of sight, hearing, smell, taste and touch during a visit to the church.

ACTIVITY TWO ······

In Maria's church you have seen that all the senses are used in worship. In some churches this is not so. When the **Society of Friends (Quakers)** meets, for example, their worship is very simple, with no taking of bread and wine and no formal prayers, readings or sermons. There is no music, no pictures, no statues, but a lot of silent **contemplation** and prayer. What kind of worship would you prefer? Explain the reasons for your views.

NOW TRY THIS ············

Look back over your work this lesson and draw up a list of useful questions that you could take to a place of worship to help you learn about it. If you have them ready, you'll always get the most from any visit and have an interesting experience.

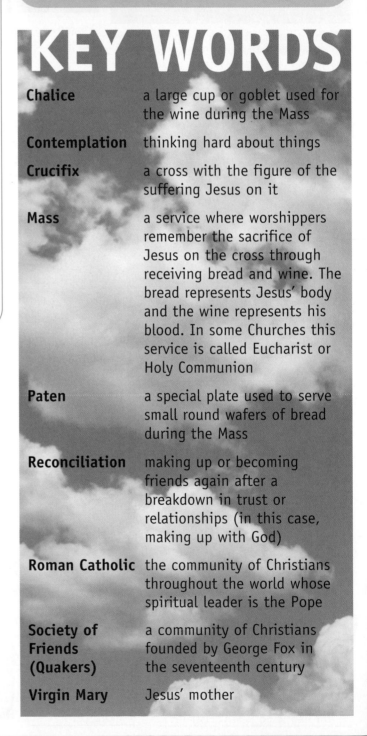

KEY WORDS

Chalice	a large cup or goblet used for the wine during the Mass
Contemplation	thinking hard about things
Crucifix	a cross with the figure of the suffering Jesus on it
Mass	a service where worshippers remember the sacrifice of Jesus on the cross through receiving bread and wine. The bread represents Jesus' body and the wine represents his blood. In some Churches this service is called Eucharist or Holy Communion
Paten	a special plate used to serve small round wafers of bread during the Mass
Reconciliation	making up or becoming friends again after a breakdown in trust or relationships (in this case, making up with God)
Roman Catholic	the community of Christians throughout the world whose spiritual leader is the Pope
Society of Friends (Quakers)	a community of Christians founded by George Fox in the seventeenth century
Virgin Mary	Jesus' mother

6. So what have you learned about religion?

SKILLS

• **thinking about** what you have learned about aspects of religion in previous lessons,
• **working out** some of the similarities and differences between religious people,
• **presenting** your findings as a poster, assembly spot, radio or TV spot or magazine article,
• **working with others** to complete your task

In previous lessons you have learned a lot to do with what religion is about. The first lesson helped you to define the word itself, introduced you to the seven aspects of religion and showed you how religion helps people to answer ultimate questions. In the second lesson you thought about how you can tell if someone is religious. You have also considered where you can see religion in the world and in the local area. Finally, you were able to learn about religion in a particular place. In this lesson you will have a chance to show how much you have learned!

You will have noticed that people from different religions have a lot in common as well as having many differences. The pictures of people worshipping in different places on the following pages will remind you of this. The rituals shown there are an outward sign of people's inward beliefs. Their beliefs have a lot in common as well as having many differences. You can read about some of their beliefs in the information section on page 19.

ACTIVITY ONE ••

In small groups choose one of the following activities to present what you have learned in this unit about religion. You should pick out at least five words from the list below and present information about each one from at least one religion. In your presentation try to show what religious people have in common, but also make it clear that there are some differences between them. The work you have done in previous lessons, together with the pictures, captions and information in this lesson on the following pages, should give you plenty of ideas.

Your presentation should be called 'What is Religion?' and it should be presented in one of the following ways:

• A poster.
• An assembly spot lasting about five minutes.
• A short radio or TV spot lasting about five minutes.
• A magazine article.

Once you have decided which one to choose, spend a few minutes writing down the things that you need to consider and include in order to make your presentation the best it can be. For example, if you choose to do a TV spot, think about a TV show of this type that you have seen. Were people with different views given an equal chance to talk? What is the role of the presenter? What makes you want to watch and listen to the show? Think about the background images, the presenter's knowledge and enthusiasm, etc.

Here are some words and phrases to get you thinking along the right lines about the content:

definition   ultimate questions   rituals   beliefs

community   feelings   right and wrong   rules

buildings   holy books   symbols   statues

clothes   food   God   similarities   differences

Zoe cheering her football team and singing the national anthem

David entering the synagogue where he listens to readings from the Torah

Abdul prays in the mosque and reads from the Qur'an

Sita and her family pray at home, and read from the Bhagavad Gita

Maria and her family go to Mass in a church, where they listen to readings from the Bible

A Sikh boy in a gurdwara where he listens to readings from the Guru Granth Sahib

A Buddhist boy meditating in a temple, where he listens to readings from the Tipitaka

ⓘ The main beliefs about God found in the major world religions:

<u>Buddhists</u> believe that people who follow the teachings and practices of the Buddha can gain **enlightenment** (true understanding of how things are) but they do not believe in a supreme god.

<u>Christians</u> believe that there is one God who has three ways of being God: God the Father (the creator of everything), God the Son (Jesus Christ) and God the **Holy Spirit** (God's active presence in the world). This idea is called the Trinity.

<u>Hindus</u> believe that there is one great power (**Brahman**) who is in and around everything. He can be approached through many different gods and ways. The many gods worshipped by Hindus represent different aspects of Brahman.

<u>Jews</u> believe that there is one God who is eternal and the creator of everything.

<u>Muslims</u> believe that there is one God, Allah, who created everything and Muhammad is his last and most important prophet.

<u>Sikhs</u> believe there is one God who is the greatest **Guru** or teacher.

NOW TRY THIS ....

You have discovered that religious people have much in common, although there are also important differences between them. Write a paragraph supporting or opposing the following statement: 'What religious people have in common is more important than their differences.'

KEY WORDS

Brahman	the one eternal reality or power for Hindus that is in everyone and everything
Enlightenment	the Buddhist term for realising the truth about life
Guru	Sikh and Hindu term for religious teacher
Holy Spirit	Christian term for God's activity in the present

SUMMARY OF UNIT 1

Lesson 2

You have learned how you might tell if someone is religious, and how deeply religious they might be.

Lesson 3

You have learned where you can see religion in the world around us and how important religious buildings might be.

Lesson 1

You have learned about the different aspects of religion, what the word 'religion' means, and how religion is about important questions in life.

What is religion?

Lesson 4

You have learned where you might see religion in the area where you live, and how to find out more about it.

Lesson 6

You have learned how religious people have some things in common; how they differ over some things too, and how to present this learning to others.

Lesson 5

You have learned what religion is like in a particular place of worship and how that place illustrates many aspects of the religion there.

UNIT 2: HOW AND WHY ARE MANY PEOPLE RELIGIOUS?

You will find out in ...

Lesson 1: Why do people belong to a particular religion?

◎ Find out the various reasons why people belong, or do not belong, to a religion.

◎ Consider in particular the importance of their family background and upbringing.

◎ Think about your own personal view on being religious and the reasons for it.

Lesson 2: Have people always been religious?

◎ Think about things that threaten our survival and how much we can control them.

◎ Find out about the things people have done since the earliest times to ensure their survival.

◎ Identify things that may threaten your own survival and ways you might try to control these.

◎ Analyse what makes an activity religious so that you can decide whether activities to ensure survival shown in this lesson mean that people have always been religious.

Lesson 3: Do people need to believe in something?

◎ Think of actions that show things that people believe.

◎ Think about the differences between 'believing' and 'believing in'.

◎ Decide what you believe about some controversial issues and argue for your beliefs.

◎ Think about beliefs that are important to you in order to produce a personal creed.

Lesson 4: Why does thinking about the origin of the world make some people religious?

◎ Think about the world and its origin and choose words to describe it.

◎ Decide how the world should be treated as a result of the words you have chosen.

◎ Identify differences between scientific and religious views of the world.

◎ Express your own views about the world and its origin.

Lesson 5: Why does thinking about being human make some people religious?

◎ Think about and discuss what it means to be human.

◎ Put the various aspects of being human into categories.

◎ Work out from short passages from the Jewish and Hindu scriptures what they believe it means to be human.

◎ Think about your own important characteristics as a human being and show this to others in the form of a badge.

Lesson 6: Why does thinking about time make some people religious?

◎ Think about and discuss the nature of time.

◎ Find out about two religious views and one non-religious view about time.

◎ Identify common features in religious calendars and discover what is happening in the major religions at the present.

◎ Express your own ideas for making the best use of time.

1. Why do people belong to a particular religion?

SKILLS

- **linking** people to religions and places,
- **sorting out** reasons why people are religious,
- **discussing** the importance of family background and upbringing,
- **finding out** more reasons for religious belief,
- **thinking about** your own reasons for being religious or not,
- **communicating** your own ideas to others

In the previous unit we looked at what we mean by religion. Now we want to ask how and why people become religious.

KEY WORDS

| **Assume** | to believe that something is true without checking it out |

ACTIVITY ONE ....

Look at pictures 1–7 on the next page. Can you tell what religion the people are just by looking at them? With a partner try to match the pictures up with the following religions – Buddhism, Christianity, Hinduism, Islam, Judaism, Sikhism, no religion.

If you have matched them up you have believed that people who look a certain way must be of a particular religion – you have **assumed**!

ACTIVITY TWO ....

Look at the map below and try to locate where the people shown in the pictures come from.

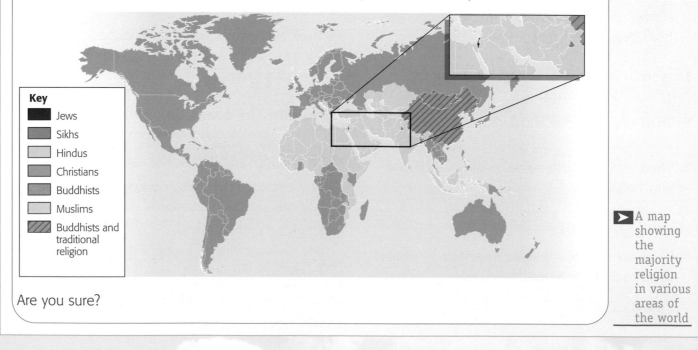

Key
- Jews
- Sikhs
- Hindus
- Christians
- Buddhists
- Muslims
- Buddhists and traditional religion

Are you sure?

➤ A map showing the majority religion in various areas of the world

You cannot assume what someone's religion is or where they live from looking at them. Most religions can be found in nearly all the countries of the world. If you live in a big city in Britain you will already be aware that all of the world's major religions can be found there.

Another reason why you cannot assume what somebody's religion is by what they look like is that people move from one religion to another. They may move for several reasons, for example: marriage, personal choice and influence from others.

ACTIVITY THREE ....

Read the quotes below about why people follow or do not follow a religion. The reasons given are very different but for many people family background and how they were brought up are very important factors.

1. With a partner, separate the quotes into two columns and put them under the headings 'Reasons related to family and upbringing' and 'Other reasons'.

2. Discuss whether you think the 'other reasons' are good reasons and be ready to share your views with the class.

ACTIVITY FOUR ....

Now think about your own views on religion. Create your own statement about why you belong or do not belong to a religion.

NOW TRY THIS ....

'You cannot choose a religion. A religion chooses you in the end.'

What do you think the person who said this meant?

Quotes from people about why they belong or do not belong to a particular religion

a) I was born and brought up in my religion. I shall never change.

b) I changed my religion when I went to university because I met some people whose religion was attractive to me.

c) I think it is important to be of the same religion as your parents, to keep the religion alive.

d) I've never thought about it.

e) You ought to marry somebody of your own religion; otherwise you create problems for your children.

f) I have no religion because I think all religions are wrong.

g) I changed my religion in order to get married.

h) I became religious after some people called at my house one day.

i) I belong to my religion because it is the religion of my country.

j) I think you should follow the religion you were brought up in.

k) I belong to two religions because my parents have different religions.

l) I used to be religious but I'm not any more.

m) I belong to my religion because it is the only one that is true.

n) I follow my religion because it helps me make sense of being alive.

o) It does not matter which religion you belong to as long as you have one.

p) I am not religious, but I read my horoscope every day.

q) I believe in my religion because it has been given to us by God as a revelation of truth.

2. Have people always been religious?

SKILLS

- **identifying** factors that threaten human survival and deciding how much control we have over them,
- **working out** what is happening in pictures,
- **interpreting** the activities shown,
- **thinking about** our own survival and preventing bad things from happening,
- **analysing** religious activities and comparing them with superstitions

We have looked at why people might or might not belong to a religion. Now we want to find out if people have always been religious.

ACTIVITY ONE ....

Water   Food   Shelter   Land   Health

What do you think this is a list of?

From the earliest times, people have tried to ensure (guarantee) their survival and basic needs by influencing nature. The pictures and information on the following pages show some of the ways they use to do this.

ACTIVITY TWO ....

Look at the pictures on the following pages.

1. Can you tell what activity is going on to try to ensure survival? With a partner, try to match the pictures with the information.

2. Make a list of the words or phrases used in the information that tell us:

   a) what basic needs people were trying to ensure, e.g. food

   b) what natural forces they were trying to influence, e.g. disease

ACTIVITY THREE ....

Now think about your life.

1. What are your basic needs today? Explain why they might be different from those in Activity One.

2. For each of the basic needs you have identified for yourself, write down anything that could threaten it. For example, your health could be threatened by pollution.

3. What do you believe in or do to try to prevent bad things from threatening you? For example, you might avoid walking under ladders.

NOW TRY THIS ....

1. How does the information on the following pages support the view that people have <u>always</u> been religious?

2. Some of the activities on the following pages might be described as **superstitions**. What is the difference in your view between religion and superstition?

KEY WORDS

Shaman	a person regarded as having access to the world of good and evil spirits
Supernatural	something beyond the ordinary, scientific, natural understanding or explanation of things
Superstition	a belief in supernatural powers bringing good or bad luck
Totem	an object believed to have spiritual power and used as an emblem by a group of people. A totem pole is a pillar on which totems are hung or carved.

ⓘ People have tried to ensure their survival by:

a) Attempting to read the future by finding out what the stars say in order to remain safe and keep away from troubles, including natural and man-made disasters.

b) Trying to keep evil spirits away from the people to keep them healthy and free from disease.

c) Praying to God as the ultimate power, or energy of life, to find out and to do his will.

d) Trying to get a good result from hunting animals so that there will be enough food to eat.

e) Understanding the powers of nature, such as earthquakes, thunder, lightning, sunshine and the sea, by linking them with a **supernatural** person or god who controls them.

f) Treating the land with reverence or respect because people depend on it for their food.

g) Using symbols to encourage people to realise that they belong to each other in the same group, and ensure their survival by sharing food and shelter, and defending themselves against their enemies.

▶ 1. A native American **totem** pole

▶ 2. Horoscopes

▶ 3. A **Shaman**

➤ 5. Ancient Greek and Roman gods

➤ 4. An Australian aborigine

➤ 6. A cave painting

People have done things like these to try to secure their future from the earliest times. There are many other ancient and modern examples – can you think of any?

➤ 7. Someone praying

3. Do people need to believe in something?

SKILLS

- **linking** beliefs to activities,
- **deciding** on your own beliefs about some issues,
- **working out** your own important beliefs,
- **arguing** for your beliefs,
- **analysing** whether beliefs can be proved

ACTIVITY ONE ....

Look at the quotes in the speech bubbles. With a partner, try to work out what the people who said these things might have been doing at the time they spoke.

You probably would not have got to school this morning unless you believed in lots of things being true already today. I bet you didn't check that your bus driver had passed their driving test or that your food had not been poisoned before you ate it! Believing things and believing in people is basic to our lives.

Believing that something is true is not quite the same as believing in a person. Can you work out the difference?

I believe that I will not fall into the water below.

I believe that I will make a full recovery.

I believe that the universe began with the big bang 15 billion years ago.

I believe that the plane will land safely in Ibiza.

I believe that my mother loves me.

I believe that God will help me in my difficult situation.

I believe that I can get an A* in French.

ACTIVITY TWO

Let's play a game!

This game will work if you move only when your teacher tells you to do so!

The four corners of your classroom will be belief points:

1. I believe.
2. I do not believe.
3. I am not sure.
4. I would like to believe but …

Your teacher will read out a statement and you must decide to move to the corner which best shows your view. (For example, 'Medical experiments on animals are wrong'.) When you get there you must quickly say to the other people in the corner why you chose that corner. Then your teacher will ask one group in one corner to try to convince another group in another corner why they should change their minds. When your teacher tells you, you will have one chance only to move to a different corner because you have changed your mind. Record the final number of pupils in each corner at the end. If you do this properly you might have time for two or three games.

When you get back to your seats, think about any conclusions that can be drawn from the game about our beliefs.

If you are still not sure of the difference between 'believing' and 'believing in', here is the answer.

ⓘ Difference between 'believing' and 'believing in':

To believe means to be sure of the truth of something, even if it cannot be proved to be true.

To believe in something or someone means to have **faith** in and trust them.

Some beliefs are deeper and more important than others. For example, believing that a penalty should have been given in a football match is not quite as important as believing that your doctor is not giving you the wrong medicine!

What are the most important things that human beings have beliefs about? What do we believe is really important in life? What people believe leads them to think that some things are more important than others. These are called their **values**. One example is that if you believe that being cruel to animals is wrong, then your values will include respect for animal rights.

Human beings have always had beliefs to try to make sense of the world around them. Some believe in **spirits** to explain how we are alive. Some believe in science as being able to explain everything. Some believe in **God** as the power behind the **universe**. Some believe in all of these. Some believe in none of these. Even believing in nothing is a belief!

ACTIVITY THREE ··········

A statement of beliefs is often called a **creed**. Write your own creed to show four important beliefs that you have.

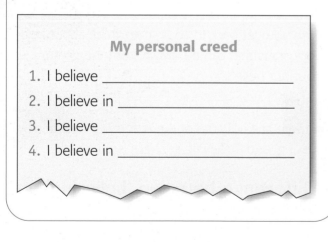

My personal creed

1. I believe _____
2. I believe in _____
3. I believe _____
4. I believe in _____

NOW TRY THIS ···········

1. Look again at the quotes in the speech bubbles on the previous two pages. With your partner, try to put the beliefs they contain into different groups – 'provable beliefs' and 'not provable beliefs'. One way to do this is to ask your partner to read each quote out loud and then say 'Prove it!'. If they can give you an answer that you could check, this means that the belief is provable. For example, 'I believe I can get an A* in French because I can prove that I have got As in my last three tests.' If it is impossible to check on, then it is not provable. Remember that beliefs may not have to be provable to be true.

2. Think about beliefs that are not provable. If you could prove a belief to be true would it still be a belief?

KEY WORDS

Creed	a statement of beliefs (from the Latin 'credo' meaning 'I believe')
Faith	complete trust or confidence
God	the power or cause behind everything
Provable	can be shown to be true beyond reasonable doubt
Spirit	energy or life in a person, animal, place or thing that some people believe exists
Universe	all that exists
Values	what people hold to be important or valuable

4. Why does thinking about the origin of the world make some people religious?

SKILLS

• **thinking** about the world and its origin,
• **choosing** adjectives to describe the world,
• **working out** the consequences of how you treat the world,
• **analysing** religious and scientific views of the world, explaining your own beliefs about the world

We have looked at the way human beings might have lots of beliefs. The reason why religious people feel that beliefs are important is because they help to give meaning to the world around them, and to their lives.

► The Earth, looking from the Moon. No human being ever saw this before 1959. What does this picture make you think about the Earth?

ACTIVITY ONE ....

Think quietly about the world around you for a moment. Ask yourself these questions:

- Where did it come from?
- Why is it here?
- Did you make the world you live in?
- Did anybody make it?

Look at the picture of the Earth on the previous page. How do you feel about it? Choose from the words on the right to describe what you think.

wonderful
unimportant
planned
ugly
designed
accident
temporary
vast
exciting
a gift
happy
sad
bad
necessary
random
free
good
tragic
beautiful
variety
created
a **right**
ours
everlasting

If people feel the world is a special place, it is likely to influence how they treat it, whether they look after it or not. How does the way you feel about the world influence the way you treat it?

ACTIVITY TWO ....

1. With a partner, look at the words you chose in Activity One to describe how you feel about the world, and try to work out how you think you ought to treat the Earth if this is the way you feel about it. For example, you could put 'Beautiful: so I look after it so it stays beautiful ...', or 'Sad: so I want to help make it a better place ...'.

2. Add your beliefs about the world to your personal creed from the last lesson.

The attitudes that Jews, Christians, Muslims and Sikhs have to the world lead them to believe in God as the Creator of the universe. They also think, along with Hindus and Buddhists, that this world is not all there is. Read the information on the next page and think carefully about it. Be aware that many scientists are religious and many religious people are scientists!

ACTIVITY THREE ....

Read the newspaper stories on the opposite page.

1. Create your own headlines to show what the main message is in each of the stories.

2. What do you think about the big bang theory? Do you think it could have happened? If so, what caused the big bang? Do you believe something else? What?

ACTIVITY FOUR ....

Design a poster to illustrate the beliefs in your personal creed. (You could draw them around a picture of the world.)

NOW TRY THIS ....

Decide whether the stories in the newspaper articles actually **contradict** one another. Is it possible to believe in one of the religious stories *and* the scientific story? Why or why not?

It started with a bang!

Scientists believe that the universe is a result of a big bang about 15 billion years ago. They're still not sure why it happened, but the Earth resulted from a cooling down of some of the debris floating round the Sun. About 5 billion years ago Earth was cool enough for water to exist; then life emerged from the water. Eventually, about 1 million years ago, modern human beings developed from previous life forms and spread over the earth forming **civilisations**.

It's just a phase we're going through!

Hindus and Buddhists say that the universe has been around for **eons** and was not the result of anybody or anything in particular. It is not permanent and it will eventually decay. Life on Earth is only one stage in a long process of escaping from this decay.

It was God!

Jews, Christians and Muslims say that the universe did not come into existence by accident, like some scientists think, but on purpose. They think some power or force is responsible for it. They call this power 'God', and believe that God wanted the universe to exist. The Earth is meant as a place for human beings to live in and to look after. It is a good place, and most of what is wrong with it is the result of human beings treating the world and each other badly.

Sikhs also believe that there is one God who is the creator of the universe and is everywhere. Human beings should all have equal status because they are all God's creation.

KEY WORDS

Civilisation	people living in a particular part of the Earth joining together and developing ways of life
Contradict	to deny the truth of something by supporting the opposite point of view
Designed	deliberately made to fit or be like it is
Eons	periods of time that are so long they have no numbers
Random	by chance, not intended
Right	something that you are entitled to, not as a privilege but as something you should have

33

5. Why does thinking about being human make some people religious?

SKILLS

- **thinking about** and discussing what it means to be human,
- **putting into categories** the various aspects of being human,
- **interpreting** what the Jewish and Hindu scriptures say about being human,
- **designing** a personal badge and explaining the reasons for your design

The most complicated things in the universe that we know about are human brains. They are not the largest of animal brains, but they are the cleverest. What is a person? What kind of creatures are we? Religious people believe that human beings are so complex and unique that they give clues to the meaning of life.

ACTIVITY ONE ......

Think of a person you know. Now answer yes or no to the following questions:

- If that person lost a finger in an accident would they still be that same person?
- If that person lost a leg in an accident would they still be that same person?
- If that person lost their head in an accident would they still be that same person?

Now, give reasons for the answers you gave. Discuss this with a partner. What conclusions do you come to?

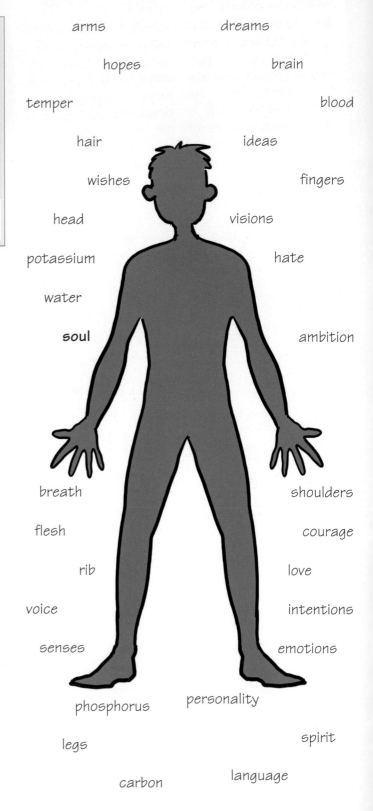

arms   dreams
hopes   brain
temper   blood
hair   ideas
wishes   fingers
head   visions
potassium   hate
water
soul   ambition
breath   shoulders
flesh   courage
rib   love
voice   intentions
senses   emotions
phosphorus   personality
legs   spirit
carbon   language

ACTIVITY TWO ·················

1. With a partner, look at the words around the picture on the left that describe some of the things that human beings are made of. Put the words into two groups to describe the body/physical, and thoughts/feelings.

2. What conclusions do you draw about what human beings are like?

ⓘ A story about people from the Jewish **scriptures**

These are words written by some Jews about 2700 years ago to describe the role of human beings:

'…the Lord God formed the man from the dust of the ground and breathed into his nostrils the breath of life, and the man became a living being. Now the Lord God had planted a garden in the east, in **Eden**; and there he put the man … to work it and take care of it … The Lord God said, "It is not good for the man to be alone. I will make a helper suitable for him." Now the Lord God had formed out of ground all the beasts of the field and all the birds of the air. He brought them to the man to see what he would name them … the Lord God caused the man to fall into a deep sleep; and while he was sleeping, he took one of the man's ribs and closed up the place with flesh. Then the Lord God made a woman from the rib.'

(From **Genesis** 2)

ACTIVITY THREE ············

Read the story from the Jewish scriptures on the left and think carefully about it. What does it say about where human beings have come from and their relationship to other living beings?

ⓘ An extract about people from the *Bhagavad Gita*, a Hindu scripture

These are words spoken by the god **Krishna** to Arjuna, the hero of the story:

'As the Spirit of our mortal body wanders on in childhood and youth and old age, the Spirit wanders on to a new body … As a man leaves an old garment and puts on one that is new, the Spirit leaves his mortal body and wanders on to one that is new.'

NOW TRY THIS ············

Read the extract from the Hindu scriptures above. What is the most important belief about human beings shown?

The way religious people feel about human beings causes them to have certain beliefs about themselves. They believe that human beings are special. The beliefs that Jews, Christians, Muslims and Sikhs have about themselves lead them to believe in God as the Creator of the universe. Hindus and Buddhists believe that human beings are intended to leave this world after being reborn in it many times, to disappear into a greater reality that is mysterious and beyond human understanding.

What do you believe about yourself?

In olden days, important people had coats of arms. These were special personal designs, like badges, that they put on their shields and flags. If they were wearing armour, especially helmets, it was impossible to recognise who they were, so putting the designs on their shields helped other people to identify them.

ACTIVITY FOUR ....

1. Think about yourself. If you had a personal badge or coat of arms, what might it contain? Create a simple badge for yourself to show four things about you.

2. Write a paragraph to explain why you chose the parts of your design.

KEY WORDS

Eden	according to the story in Genesis, the perfect place or garden where human beings were originally put by God to enjoy the world, but from which they were expelled when they disobeyed him
Genesis	first Book of the Jewish Torah and the Christian Bible
Krishna	one of the most popular of the Hindu gods who came to earth in human form
Scripture	a piece of writing, a text or a book regarded as very special or sacred
Soul	the spiritual part of a human being, often regarded as the part of them that never dies, that is, immortal

NOW TRY THIS ......

Write a paragraph about what you think it means to be human. Include something about the origin of human life, relationships with other living beings and the purpose of life.

> This coat of arms was for Diana, Princess of Wales. How do you think it shows her royal status?

6. Why does thinking about time make some people religious?

SKILLS

• **thinking** about and discussing how people understand time,
• **interpreting** some ideas from religious and non-religious people about time,
• **finding** common features in religious calendars,
• **identifying** what happens at a certain time of year for religious people,
• **expressing** your own ideas about making the best use of time

One of the things that interests human beings is time. You might be wearing a watch, or there may be a clock in your classroom. Just spend a minute watching it. The closer you look, the slower it seems to be going. Another thing to note is that the time you spend looking at the clock is time you will never have again. It is like water flowing under a bridge. Once it has passed, it is gone for ever.

Time passes regularly even though sometimes it seems to go faster than at other times. Rainy days always seem longer than sunny ones and time in school goes slower than time at parties!

These lines both represent time. What does each say about it?

Story of the bird

About 1000 years ago, a king was holding a party in a huge stone hall with windows high up in the walls. Suddenly a little bird flew in a window on one side of the hall, then flew out of a window on the other side, never to be seen again. This made the king stop his partying. Where had the bird come from? Where had the bird gone? Nobody knew! The king thought that this was like his life. Where had he been before he was born? Nobody knew! Where would he go when he died? Nobody knew! All they knew was that once they had died they would be gone for ever! For the king, who became a Christian, the story of the bird was the story of a lifetime on earth.

ⓘ Most Jews, Christians and Muslims believe that each person has only one life on earth. Each person is a gift of God and goes back to God, if they lead a good life on Earth.

Darkness

A famous philosopher called David Hume, who did not believe in God, once said that he was no more puzzled by the darkness into which he was going than by the darkness from which he came.

ⓘ Most humanists and non-religious people believe that a person comes from nowhere and goes nowhere. Death is the end of life.

Changing clothes

'As a man leaves an old garment and puts on one that is new, the Spirit leaves his mortal body and wanders on to one that is new.'

(From the *Bhagavad Gita* 2:22)

ⓘ Most Hindus, Buddhists and Sikhs believe that each person may have many lives, for, when a person dies, that person is reborn (**reincarnated**) as a new living thing. This goes on until the person becomes so good that they escape from the circle of life and death.

ACTIVITY TWO ••••••••••••••

The three extracts above show ways of looking at time. You have to read them and represent them by drawing a diagram for each. One story will be represented by a circle and the other two will be represented by straight lines.

1. Draw a circle and two straight lines.

2. Read the stories that you think can be represented by straight lines again and then for each story write where they tell you time comes from and where it goes to at the ends of the straight lines.

3. Write the following labels on each of the three diagrams to show you how life develops: birth, childhood, adulthood, old age, death.

4. Write the following title above your diagrams: Three ideas of lifetime

5. Write a sentence to say which of the diagrams you agree with most and why.

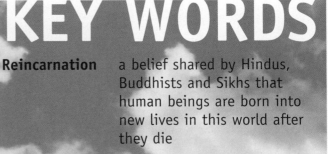

KEY WORDS

Reincarnation a belief shared by Hindus, Buddhists and Sikhs that human beings are born into new lives in this world after they die

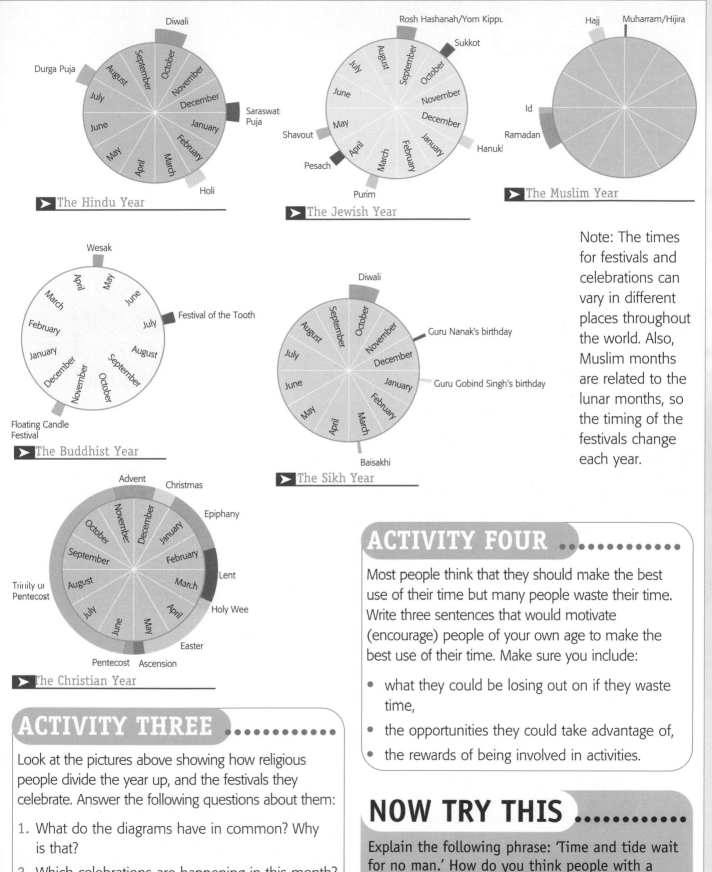

Diwali
September
August
July
June
May
April
March
February
January
December
November
October
Durga Puja
Saraswati Puja
Holi

> The Hindu Year

Rosh Hashanah/Yom Kippur
Sukkot
August
July
June
May
April
March
February
January
December
November
October
September
Shavout
Pesach
Purim
Hanukl

> The Jewish Year

Hajj
Muharram/Hijira
Id
Ramadan

> The Muslim Year

Note: The times for festivals and celebrations can vary in different places throughout the world. Also, Muslim months are related to the lunar months, so the timing of the festivals change each year.

Wesak
April
May
March
June
February
July
January
August
December
September
November
October
Festival of the Tooth
Floating Candle Festival

> The Buddhist Year

Diwali
September
August
July
June
May
April
March
February
January
December
November
October
Guru Nanak's birthday
Guru Gobind Singh's birthday
Baisakhi

> The Sikh Year

Advent
Christmas
November
December
January
October
September
February
August
March
July
April
June
May
Epiphany
Lent
Holy Wee
Easter
Ascension
Pentecost
Trinity or Pentecost

> The Christian Year

ACTIVITY THREE ....

Look at the pictures above showing how religious people divide the year up, and the festivals they celebrate. Answer the following questions about them:

1. What do the diagrams have in common? Why is that?

2. Which celebrations are happening in this month?

ACTIVITY FOUR ....

Most people think that they should make the best use of their time but many people waste their time. Write three sentences that would motivate (encourage) people of your own age to make the best use of their time. Make sure you include:

• what they could be losing out on if they waste time,

• the opportunities they could take advantage of,

• the rewards of being involved in activities.

NOW TRY THIS ....

Explain the following phrase: 'Time and tide wait for no man.' How do you think people with a religious belief would interpret this phrase?

SUMMARY OF UNIT 2

Lesson 2

You have learned that people have always had important reasons for being religious, connected with trying to ensure their survival.

Lesson 3

You have learned that all people have beliefs about themselves and the world because of their wish to explain what things are like, and why.

Lesson 1

You have learned how people may belong, or not belong, to religions for many reasons, including where they are born, how they are brought up and by their own personal choice.

How and why are many people religious?

Lesson 4

You have learned that, for religious people, thinking about the origin of the world means that they hold particular beliefs to explain why it is here, and how they should look after it.

Lesson 6

You have learned that religious people have different beliefs about time and how it should be used, and how the passage of time is celebrated during the year in different festivals.

Lesson 5

You have learned that, for religious people, thinking about what it means to be human leads them to have particular beliefs about what humans are like, and why.

UNIT 3: WHERE HAVE THE RELIGIONS OF THE WORLD COME FROM AND HOW ARE THEY LINKED?

You will find out in ...

Lesson 1: Where did Judaism, Christianity and Islam come from?

◎ Find out where Judaism, Christianity and Islam all began.

◎ Show understanding of why these religions developed from there.

◎ Think about what makes an inspiring leader and present ideas about this in an advertisement for a new religious leader.

Lesson 2: Where did Hinduism, Buddhism and Sikhism come from?

◎ Think about why places are special to people.

◎ Find out and explain why some places are special in Hinduism, Buddhism and Sikhism.

◎ Communicate to a friend why a place is special to you in a postcard message.

◎ Work out what pilgrims might gain from visiting places where their religion began.

Lesson 3: What about other religions?

◎ Decide how you could find out about other religions and make up some questions you could ask about them.

◎ Use pictures and information about the Zoroastrian, Jain and Baha'i faiths and work out answers to your questions.

◎ Think about the experience of belonging to a minority group.

◎ Find out about a small, local religious group (optional).

Lesson 4: What about non-religious groups?

◎ Find out the meaning of key words related to non-religious belief and identify common factors in them.

◎ Show knowledge and understanding of the main events and beliefs in the lives of influential non-religious people by planning a short film.

◎ Think about the challenge of putting across minority views.

Lesson 5: How do religious people get on with each other?

◎ Think about the amount of conflict in your own life.

◎ Develop a knowledge and understanding of the reasons for religious conflict.

◎ Consider ways of achieving harmony between religious groups.

◎ Show you know what it takes to bring an end to a struggle.

Lesson 6: How do religious people get on with each other around here?

◎ Devise questions to find out about the relationship between religious and non-religious groups in the local area.

◎ Compose a letter or e-mail to invite guests to a meeting about this.

◎ Organise a Question and Answer forum and record and present the outcome of the meeting.

Where have the religions of the world come from and how are they linked?

1. Where did Judaism, Christianity and Islam come from?

SKILLS

- finding out where Judaism, Christianity and Islam began and why, making sense of this by linking parts of sentences together,
  - making comparisons and identifying common factors,
  - expressing ideas about what makes an inspiring leader,
  - discussing why people join a new religion

We have looked at what we mean by religion, and have discovered that there are many religions in the world. We have also thought about why people are religious. Now we are going to find out where religions have come from, beginning with three religions that began in the Middle East.

ACTIVITY ONE ....

Although some religions are still the main religion in the area of the world where they began, all have spread to other parts of the world, just like many families. This activity will help you to realise this.

Once your teacher has labelled parts of the classroom as A, B, C, D and E, do the following:

- All those born in the local area (town or county), go to A.
- All those born outside this area, go to B.
- All those in A with a parent born outside the area, go to C.
- All those in A with a grandparent born outside the local area, go to D.
- Anyone born or with a parent or grandparent born outside Britain go to E.

What does this tell you about your families? How can you link this to the spread of religion?

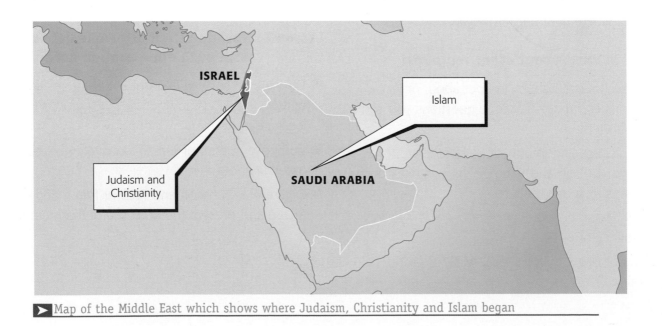

> Map of the Middle East which shows where Judaism, Christianity and Islam began

ⓘ Where and why Judaism, Christianity and Islam began

Judaism began about 4000 years ago in a land called Canaan, now called Israel. Jews believe that they are descendants of Abraham. Abraham did not worship many gods and make human **sacrifices** like those around him, but worshipped one God. God promised Abraham that he would have a land for himself and his descendants and that he would become the father of a great nation. He was led to Canaan, the 'Promised Land'. Some 500 years later Moses received the law (Torah) from God on Mount Sinai. Jews have tried to follow this throughout the centuries. Jews have suffered much **persecution** so many Jews left their land. Judaism has spread throughout the world. Today there are about 18 million Jews.

Christianity also began in Israel (then called Palestine) after the death of Jesus of Nazareth in about 30CE. Jesus was a Jewish teacher who was put to death by being nailed to a cross. Christians believe that he rose from the dead and was the Son of God, sent to save people from their sins.

Christians only believe in one God. Christianity was spread quickly by Jesus' followers, including St Paul. It came to Rome and beyond in its first hundred years, which was when the New Testament was written. It is now found all over the world, and today one in three people in the world call themselves Christian.

Islam began in the country we now call Saudi Arabia when the **prophet** Muhammad started preaching in about 611CE. Muhammad was influenced by both Judaism and Christianity. Muslims believe in one God, Allah, and that Muhammad was his last prophet. However, they believe that Allah sent many other prophets, including Ibrahim (Abraham), Musa (Moses) and 'Isa (Jesus). When he was meditating in a cave at Hira, Muhammad had a vision of the Angel Jibril (Gabriel), who asked him to recite words from Allah. These words later became the Qur'an, the Muslim holy book. When Muhammad died in 632CE, most of Arabia had accepted Islam. It soon spread to other parts of the Middle East and North Africa. Today there are nearly 2 billion Muslims across the world.

ACTIVITY TWO ••

When you have looked at the information on these pages, find the correct tails to complete the heads below.

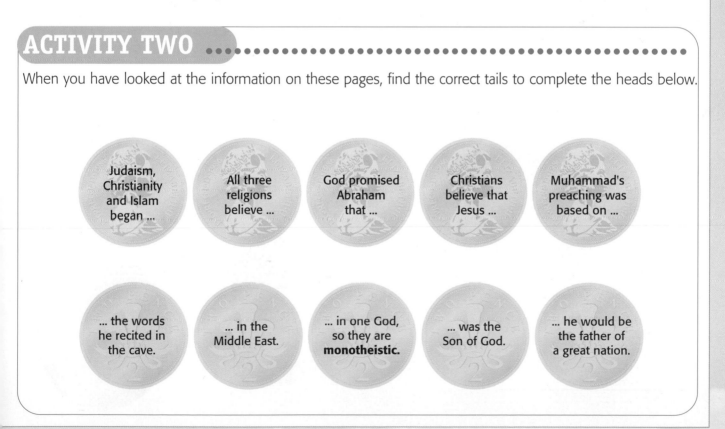

Judaism, Christianity and Islam began …

All three religions believe …

God promised Abraham that …

Christians believe that Jesus …

Muhammad's preaching was based on …

… the words he recited in the cave.

… in the Middle East.

… in one God, so they are **monotheistic.**

… was the Son of God.

… he would be the father of a great nation.

An important reason for the growth of Judaism, Christianity and Islam was the inspiring leaders. An example of an inspiring leader in the twentieth century was Martin Luther King. He campaigned for equal rights for black Americans. He was a brilliant speaker, showed great determination and was strengthened by his firm Christian faith. You can see pictures of him and other famous leaders on this page. What do you think makes someone an inspiring leader?

▶ Martin Luther King on a campaign. Do you think he looks like a leader in this photograph?

KEY WORDS

Monotheism	belief in one God
Persecution	the consistently bad treatment of an individual or group of people
Prophet	for Jews and Christians, it is a spokesperson for God; for Muslims, an honoured messenger of Allah
Sacrifice	an act of killing an animal or person as an offering to a god; or giving something up out of devotion

NOW TRY THIS ....

What do you think makes people adopt a new religion? Discuss this question with a partner and be ready to share your ideas with the rest of the class.

ACTIVITY THREE ···

Create a job advertisement for a religious leader of a new or existing religion wanting to grow. You could include these headings: 'personal qualities' (the skills they need to have), 'previous experience' (what they need to have done before and what qualifications they have) and 'role' (what their tasks will be in the new job). Below are some examples.

▶ Elizabeth I

Personal qualities: clever, ruthless, persuasive

Personal experience: public speaking, languages: Greek and Latin

Role: Queen of England – rule England and change laws to benefit the people

▶ Winston Churchill

Personal qualities: leadership, good speaker

Personal experience: in the military, author, member of political party

Role: British Prime Minister – lead on political and military issues in the UK

▶ Mother Teresa

Personal qualities: caring, patient, devoted

Personal experience: member of Catholic faith

Role: Nun – helping the sick and poor

2. Where did Hinduism, Buddhism and Sikhism come from?

SKILLS

• finding out where and why Hinduism, Buddhism and Sikhism began,
• explaining why some places are special to Hindus, Buddhists and Sikhs,
• sorting information about the beginnings of the three religions into similarities and differences,
• analysing what pilgrims gain from visiting special places in their religion,
• thinking about and expressing ideas about why places are special to you

KEY WORDS

Buddha	the 'enlightened' or awakened one; the name given to Siddhartha Gautama
Guru Granth Sahib	the collection of Sikh scriptures given its final form by the tenth Guru, Guru Gobind Singh
Sanskrit	the ancient sacred language of the Hindu scriptures

Last lesson we looked at where Judaism, Christianity and Islam came from. We saw that they began very near to each other and are connected. Now we are going to look at three more very important religions that began in a different part of the world and find out about special places linked to where Hinduism, Buddhism and Sikhism came from.

ACTIVITY ONE .....

What makes places special to you? Discuss this question in groups and be ready to share your ideas with the rest of the class.

> Pilgrims bathing in the River Ganges at Varanasi. Find the river on the map on the next page. Why do you think these people have come to bathe in this river. What do you think the atmosphere would be like there?

45

➤ The River Indus, where some of the first Hindus settled

➤ Lumbini, where the Buddha (Siddhartha Gautama) was born

Amritsar

PUNJAB

River Indus

Lumbini

River Ganges

Varanasi

Bodh Gaya

INDIA

Arabian Sea

Bay Of Bengal

Key
✳ Hindu, Buddhist and Sikh pilgrimage sites

➤ Bodh Gaya, where Siddhartha Gautama became the enlightened one (the Buddha)

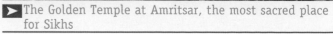

➤ The Golden Temple at Amritsar, the most sacred place for Sikhs

Date	Event	
2500BCE	Development of a civilisation near the River Indus.	HINDUISM
1500BCE	The first Hindus settled in the Indus valley. They had a great respect for nature, so the Indus and the Ganges became sacred rivers.	HINDUISM
1200BCE	Stories and ideas about many different gods representing aspects of the one Great Power, Brahman, began to be written down in **Sanskrit**.	HINDUISM
563BCE	Siddhartha Gautama, the **Buddha**, was born as a prince, in Lumbini, now in Nepal. He was influenced by Hindu teachers and later found the truth about the meaning of life when he meditated under a tree at Bodh Gaya. He gained 'enlightenment' and taught his ideas to others.	BUDDHISM
487BCE	The Buddha died. By then many in India followed his teachings.	BUDDHISM
380BCE	Gradually Buddhism split into two groups, the Theravada and Mahayana Buddhists.	BUDDHISM
From 1100CE	Islam became a big influence in India.	
1469CE	Guru Nanak was born at Talwandi in the Punjab and, when he was 30, God's message was revealed to him. He began to teach about belief in one god and that religion is not as important as the way you live your life.	SIKHISM
1539–1708CE	Nine more gurus followed Guru Nanak but the last, Guru Gobind Singh, said that a book, called the **Guru Granth Sahib**, could teach them from now on. Very old copies are kept at the Golden Temple in Amritsar.	SIKHISM
From 1700CE	British and French Christian rule became a a big influence in India.	
Today	There are about 790 million Hindus in India, and half a million Hindus in the UK.	HINDUISM
	There are about 360 million Buddhists around the world, mostly in South and East Asia, with 150,000 in the UK.	BUDDHISM
	Sikhs are found all over the world, numbering about 16 million, with 330,000 in the UK.	SIKHISM

ACTIVITY TWO ....•••••••••••••

Look at the timeline and the pictures on the left. Then try to work out which of the places below are special to Hindus, Buddhists and Sikhs and why.

1. Valley of the River Indus
2. Lumbini
3. Bodh Gaya
4. Punjab
5. Amritsar

ACTIVITY THREE ••••••••••••

Write a postcard you might send to a friend about a place that is special to you. Try to explain why the place is special in your message.

Pilgrims are people who make special journeys for religious reasons. Pilgrims in the religions studied in this lesson and the previous one try to visit special places associated with the origins of their religion.

ACTIVITY FOUR ••••••••••••

1. Use the pictures on pages 45 and 46 to help you choose three words that could describe how you might feel if you visited these special places.
2. What do you think religious people gain from visiting places that are special to them? Present your ideas in a spider diagram.

NOW TRY THIS ••••••••••

With a partner, produce a table to show similarities and differences in the development of these religions. Put similarities in one column of your table and differences in the other.

3. What about other religions?

SKILLS

• **deciding** how you can find out about other religions and making up questions to ask about them,
• **matching** pictures with the correct information,
• **finding out** the answers to your questions from the information,
• **thinking about** what it is like to belong to a small group and particularly a religious group,
• **researching** a small local religion and presenting the findings as a poster or collage

We have looked at where the six major world religions have come from and why. All of them can be found in Britain. Now we are going to do the same for other religions and beliefs that might be local to you.

The table below shows you three religions that we have not looked at so far.

Examples of other religions or beliefs, some of which may be local to you:

Church of the Latter Day Saints

Liberal

Shia

Reform

Hasidic

Christadelphianism

Seventh Day Adventists

Sufism

Hare Krishna movement

	Zoroastrianism	Jainism	Baha'i
When it began	Tenth century BCE	Sixth century BCE	Nineteenth century CE
Where it began	Borders of Afghanistan and Iran	Bihar, India	Iran
Name of the founder	**Zarathustra**	**Mahavira** ('Great Hero')	Muirza Husayn Ali Nuri, known as The Glory of God or **Baha'Allah**
Number in modern world	About 150,000	Between 2 and 3 million	About 2 million
Links with other religions	Influenced Judaism, Christianity and Islam.	Developed from Hinduism and shares some beliefs with Buddhism.	Developed from beliefs in the branch of Islam known as Shia.
Key beliefs	Belief in one God, **Ahura Mazda** ('Wise Lord'). He fathered twin spirits who had to choose between good and evil. One chose good and the other chose evil. This choice exists for every person in their life. Belief that one day human beings will have pure bodies in a new life after this life.	Belief in a creator, but Jainists think of the universe as a huge person with humans at its waist. The soul must try to rise through the heavens to the top of the universe where it will be still and free from pain. Belief in 'ahimsa'. This means non-injury to other living things. Monks and nuns tread softly to avoid crushing insects and may wear masks and avoid drinking water so that they don't kill insects.	Belief in Baha'Allah, who followed the teachings of Sayyid'Ali Muhammad, (known as the '**Bab**' or 'Gate'), who believed in the coming of a saviour. Belief that other religions of the world are not wrong, but stages on the way to the truth, stressing the importance of equality, non-violence and care for humanity.

ACTIVITY ONE ••••••••••••

With a partner, decide on six questions that you could ask a member of a religion to find out more about it.

ACTIVITY TWO ••••••••••••

Choose one of the religions in the table on the previous page and see if you can find any answers to the questions you decided to ask in Activity One.

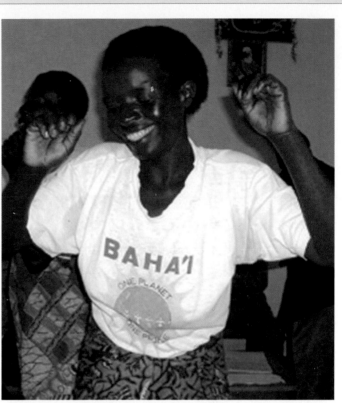

▶ A baha'i follower. How does this photo reflect what you know about this religion?

▶ A Jain wearing a mask to prevent the accidental death of an insect. Try to remember what this shows a belief in. (Clue: it begins with the letter 'a'.)

▶ A Zoroastrian, introducing a boy to the faith. What other religions can you think of which have initiation (or introduction) ceremonies?

ACTIVITY THREE ●●

What do you think it feels like to be a member of a small religion?

EITHER:

1. Write about a time in your life when you have been a member of a small group such as a sports team or drama group. (You could write about why you were in the group, and what it felt like to be one of a small number of people. Was it good to be in a small rather than a large group?)

OR:

2. Write a list of the advantages and disadvantages you think there might be of being a member of a small religious group.

Try to show that you understand what it feels like to be in a **minority**.

NOW TRY THIS ●●●●●●●●●●●

What do you think makes some religious people join a small group rather than a large one? Discuss this question in groups and be ready to share your ideas with the rest of the class.

An extra challenge!

If you have the opportunity, try to find out about one of the small religious groups in your local community. It may be one of the religions in the list on page 48, one of the three religions you have looked at this lesson, or a different group. Use the ideas and questions you came up with in Activity One to help you. Resources in your school and library, including ICT resources, will be helpful. You might even know someone who belongs to one of these groups locally and you could talk to them.

Produce a poster or collage of information about the local religion that you have found out about. Be sure to indicate its main beliefs and practices.

KEY WORDS

Bab	'Gate', a title applied to Sayyid Ali Muhammad (1819-1850), a religious leader executed in Persia whose teachings inspired the founder of the Baha'i faith
Baha'Allah	Muirza Husayn Ali Nuri (1817-1892), the founder of the Baha'i faith
Ahura Mazda	literally 'Wise Lord', the god worshipped in Zoroastrianism
Mahavira	'Great Hero', the founder of Jainism
Minority	a group of people which is small in relation to the larger group around them
Zarathustra	the founder of the Zoroastrian religion

4. What about non-religious groups?

SKILLS

- **finding out** the meaning of words that are specifically linked to non-religious beliefs and identifying common factors in the words,
- **planning** a short film to show understanding of important events and beliefs in the life of a famous non-religious person,
- **thinking about** the challenges involved in belonging to a non-religious group

ACTIVITY ONE ·················

The logos below show you some of the organisations in Britain that have beliefs but would not want to be thought of as religious. Some of them are described as 'humanist'. There is a description of humanism below. Look up the other words in their titles which the arrows point to and find the meanings. What do these words have in common?

ⓘ Humanism

This is a belief that people can live good lives without religious or superstitious beliefs. People should make the best of the life they have, by creating their own meaning and purpose for it because they are not being guided by a religion. People should take responsibility for their own actions and work with others for the common good. Morals are based on experience only and not religious belief.

We have looked at where religions found in Britain have come from and why. Many people are not religious, but may have strong beliefs. They may show these beliefs in their practices.

Names of secular (non-religious) or humanist groups

Humanist Philosopher's Group

SOUTH PLACE ETHICAL SOCIETY

International Humanist and Ethical Union

Rationalist Press Association

BRITISH HUMANIST ASSOCIATION
for the one life we have

National Secular Society

ⓘ Some influential non-religious people

Charles Darwin 1809–82

Charles Darwin was born in Shropshire and studied medicine at Edinburgh University and biology at Cambridge University. From 1831–36 he was a naturalist (studying how plants and animals formed over time) on HMS Beagle, which was making a scientific survey of South American waters. From 1841 he spent his time at Downe in Kent concentrating on his garden and breeding pigeons and chickens. He also wrote several scientific books including the famous *The Origin of Species* in 1859. Many Christians thought that his theory about evolution (how living beings developed) challenged the truth of the story of creation in the Bible. There were angry debates between Darwin's supporters and some leading Christians about this.

Charles Bradlaugh 1833–91

Charles Bradlaugh was born in London. From an early age he began to question Christianity and left home after disagreements with his father in 1849. He became a famous lecturer on secular (non-religious) ideas and started the National Secular Society in 1866. He was elected MP for Northampton in 1880, but refused to take an oath on the Bible to allow him to take his seat in parliament. Instead he requested to 'affirm', which is a non-religious way of doing this. He had to go through the election process three times until a new Speaker of the House of Commons accepted that he be allowed to take his seat after making a 'non-religious affirmation'. In 1888 his Oaths Act enabled non-religious affirmations to be given as an alternative to the religious oaths.

Bertrand Russell 1872–1970

Bertrand Russell was born in Wales and became a famous philosopher and mathematician. He became a lecturer at Cambridge University in 1895. He was turned down as a Liberal MP in 1907 because he was too 'free-thinking'. He refused to fight in the First World War and went to prison for six months in 1918. He believed that questions about God were not sensible ones to ask, since he believed that there was no god. He wrote about politics, religion and education. In 1950 he won the Nobel Prize for Literature. He became a campaigner in favour of getting rid of nuclear weapons, and led many demonstrations.

ACTIVITY TWO ·····•••••••••••

1. In small groups, imagine that you are producing a short film about the life of one of the figures on the previous page. Decide on the three scenes that you would include in your film and why. (You could do some more research on the person you have chosen.) Decide on the characters to be included, the scenery or setting, the action taking place and the stage directions. Plan your film in the form of a flow diagram. Be sure to indicate the main beliefs and practices of the people you choose. For example:

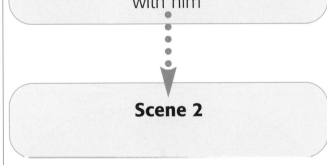

Scene 1

(Characters) Darwin and Captain

(Scenery) 1831–36 aboard HMS Beagle

(Setting) Off the coast of South America

(Action) Captain enters to discuss Darwin's thoughts about evolution with him

Scene 2

2. Act out one of the scenes from your film for the rest of the class. One of the group should give a short introduction to the scene so that everyone will understand where it fits into the story.

ACTIVITY THREE ·····•••••••••

What do you think it feels like to be an individual who has to struggle against others to get their point of view across and be accepted?

EITHER:

1. Write a letter to a friend describing what happened when you had to do this at some time in your life so far.

OR:

2. Write a list of what might encourage a person in such a struggle.

NOW TRY THIS ·····•••••••

1. What do you think makes some people join a humanist group? Write about your ideas and explain them fully. Try to refer to examples from the lives of the people studied in this lesson.

2. Many famous people in modern times say they are humanists, **agnostics** or **atheists**. They include Katharine Hepburn, Charlie Chaplin, George Bernard Shaw, Clare Rayner, Linda Smith and Terry Pratchett. Try to find out more about their views.

KEY WORDS

Agnostic	someone who doubts the existence of a god or gods
Atheist	someone who does not believe in a god or gods

You should also have discovered the meaning of **humanist**, **ethical**, **secular**, **philosopher** and **rationalist** during this lesson!

5. How do religious people get on with each other?

SKILLS

- **working out** some reasons for religious conflict,
- **finding out** how religious peace and harmony may be achieved,
- **thinking about** conflict in your own life, expressing your own ideas on this

Very often the differences between religious people are not about religion, but about something else that causes a religious division, for example political power, land or rights.

We have looked at a large variety of the religions and other beliefs in this country. They have not always got on well with each other in the past, and there are places in the world where people still do not seem to get on with each other. This is even true in Britain at times.

ACTIVITY ONE ••••••••••••••

Think about your own life. Estimate what percentage of time you spend arguing or fighting each day.

Hopefully you will have realised that disagreements take up only a very small amount of your time, and that for the rest of the time you get on well with people. This is the same for religious groups. But here are examples of times when they haven't got on well with each other, and they have been in **conflict**.

ACTIVITY TWO ••••••••••••

The diagrams show you some of the times and places when religious groups have not got on with each other.

1. Which example is the odd one out? Explain why. You may find more than one.

2. Make a list of different reasons why there have been conflicts and persecution.

3. Why do you think some people might try to discriminate against others?

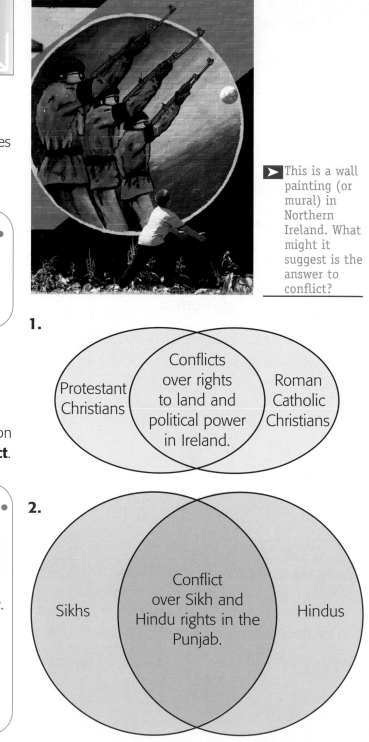

▶ This is a wall painting (or mural) in Northern Ireland. What might it suggest is the answer to conflict?

1.

Protestant Christians — Conflicts over rights to land and political power in Ireland. — Roman Catholic Christians

2.

Sikhs — Conflict over Sikh and Hindu rights in the Punjab. — Hindus

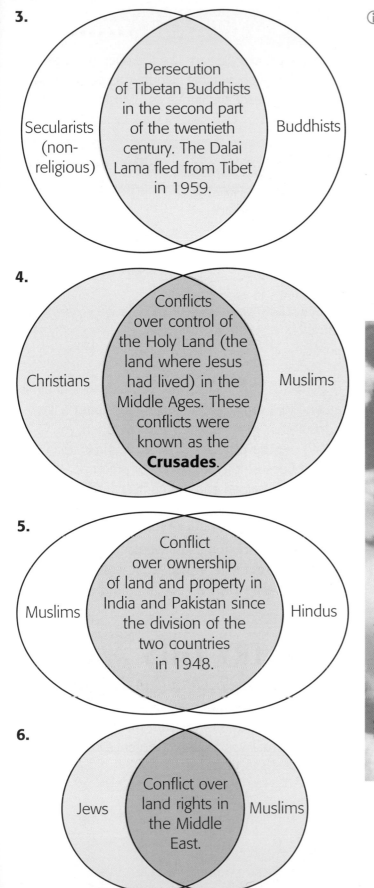

3.

Secularists (non-religious) — Persecution of Tibetan Buddhists in the second part of the twentieth century. The Dalai Lama fled from Tibet in 1959. — Buddhists

4.

Christians — Conflicts over control of the Holy Land (the land where Jesus had lived) in the Middle Ages. These conflicts were known as the **Crusades**. — Muslims

5.

Muslims — Conflict over ownership of land and property in India and Pakistan since the division of the two countries in 1948. — Hindus

6.

Jews — Conflict over land rights in the Middle East. — Muslims

ⓘ Religious prejudice in Britain

A few people are **prejudiced** against Muslims. They sometimes damage mosques or other property. This is sometimes called **Islamophobia**.

A few people are also prejudiced against Jews because they have **stereotypical** views about them. Sometimes, for example, they damage Jewish graves and synagogues. This is called **anti-Semitism**.

Members of other religions and ethnic groups are also sometimes victims of **discrimination**. However, for most of the time people live in safety and are very tolerant of each other.

KEY WORDS

Anti-Semitism	hostility to or prejudice against Jews
Conflict	an argument about something that may develop into a row and become violent
Crusade	a strong campaign against a person, group or practice that you think is mistaken
Discrimination	making an unfair distinction in the way you treat groups of people or individuals
Islamophobia	irrational fear or dislike of Muslims
Prejudice	an unfair opinion that is not based on reason or experience
Stereotypical	assuming ideas about people, based on a standard image, without knowing the truth

ⓘ Tolerance and harmony between religions

There are many examples of different religious groups working together so that people of different cultures and faiths can live in peace and harmony. In the UK, groups such as the *Inter Faith Network* and the *Three Faiths Forum* have been set up to work for good relations among different religious communities.

Elsewhere in the world an example of someone who worked for religious harmony in the last century was *Mahatma Gandhi*. He was a Hindu who believed that there was much truth in other religions. He wanted to achieve equal rights for people in South Africa and India. He hated violence because he thought it created more problems than it solved. He prevented violence between Hindus and Muslims in India in 1947 by threatening to starve himself to death unless the violence stopped. Gandhi's example has inspired many religious and non-religious people throughout the world to work for peace and harmony between different groups.

➤ Mahatma Gandhi, who once said, 'An eye for an eye and the world would be blind'. What do you think he meant by this?

ACTIVITY THREE ....

Create your own diagram like the ones on pages 54 and 55 to show what Gandhi was prepared to do to bring peace to Hindus and Muslims in India.

ACTIVITY FOUR ....

In times of non-violence, there is peace. Write an acrostic for the word

P

E

A

C

E

using words and phrases that you think would bring an end to a struggle. You could think about a time or conflict in your life when you (or others you know) may have been bullied or discriminated against because of your beliefs or practices. What would have helped end the conflict in that situation? Or you might think about a conflict on a world scale and what would have helped to bring world peace. Pick some key words to use in your acrostic. For example, would 'education' have helped to 'end violence'.

NOW TRY THIS ....

What do you think makes some people want to be violent over religious matters? Write a paragraph to explain your views and suggest some alternatives to using violence to settle religious disagreements.

6. How do religious people get on with each other around here?

SKILLS

- **thinking** up questions to ask about religious and non-religious groups in the local area, composing a letter or e-mail to invite guests,
- **organising** a meeting with leaders of faith communities,
- **recording and presenting** the outcome of the meeting to others,
- **thinking about** your own ideas for good relations and explaining them

ⓘ Object of the lesson

The object of this lesson is for you to find out the information for yourself! Activity One helps you to find out about faiths in your area. Activities Two and Three ask you to think about creating better relationships between faiths.

We have looked at a large variety of religions and other beliefs in this country. They have not always got on well with each other in the past, and there are places in the world where they still do not seem to get on with each other.

Think about your own community or local area. What do you know about the relationships among the different religions there? You might find you know little. If so, think about how you might find out more.

One way you might find out is to invite leaders from the various religious and other groups in your area to a Question and Answer **forum** in your class or school where you could find out about the different faiths.

If you were going to do this, you would need to compose a polite letter or e-mail to them, explaining why you are inviting them and giving examples of the kind of questions they might expect to be asked.

STUDENT SACRE CONFERANCE ON 30TH JUNE 2004

AT FUTURE HOUSE BRADFORD

➤ This is an example of a forum that was organised by young people in Bradford to help them gain a better understanding of different faiths in their area

ACTIVITY ONE ··················

Compose a letter or e-mail to a local religious leader. Think about the appropriate beginning and ending for your letter or e-mail and the subject of your questions. You might want to ask about any joint activities between the different religions and groups, who the groups that meet are, and how often they meet.

ACTIVITY TWO ···················

1. Draw a diagram to show how you would set up a room for the forum – decide how the chairs and table should be arranged, what decoration or designs should be shown around the room and what order or places people should sit in.

2. Decide who is to chair the forum and why.

3. Draw up a code of conduct for the visitors and for the audience to explain how they should behave during the forum.

NOW TRY THIS ············

Think of suggestions you would like to make to encourage a good relationship between the different religious groups in your area. Make a list of suggestions and explain your reasons. Examples might include a directory of religious groups or co-operation between religious groups to carry out a local project.

Write a press release to advertise an Inter Faith event to say what you hope will happen.

▶ Religious leaders at Assisi, where they agreed on the importance of looking after the world and environment

Here are two examples of how different faiths come together at an international level.

▶ Religious leaders at Remembrance Day

Logos of inter-faith and inter-religious organisations in the UK

▶ The Three Faiths Forum brings together representatives of Judaism, Christianity and Islam

The Inter Faith Network for the United Kingdom

▶ The Inter Faith Network helps different religious groups work together

This is an example on a national level where the government tries to ensure that young people are aware of different faiths around them through their learning at school. Here, Charles Clarke, who was the Education Minister, is launching the new RE Framework.

Here are some examples of inter-faith projects at a local level. What do you think they might be talking about?

KEY WORDS

Forum	a place, time or event for joint talks and discussions
Inter-faith	discussions and activities held jointly between people who belong to different religious faiths, with the aim of achieving greater understanding and co-operation
Inter-religious	looking across one or more religions to try to produce greater understanding
SACRE	a group of people who have responsibility for religious education in each local area in England and Wales (Standing Advisory Council for Religious Education)

SUMMARY OF UNIT 3

Lesson 2

You have learned where Hinduism, Buddhism and Sikhism came from, how they developed and the important role of special places.

Lesson 3

You have learned about minority religions such as Zoroastrianism, Jainism and the Baha'i faith, as well as about what belonging to a small minority group might be like.

Lesson 1

You have learned where Judaism, Christianity and Islam came from, how they developed and the important role of inspiring leaders.

Where have the religions of the world come from and how are they linked?

Lesson 4

You have learned about non-religious groups and how humanism developed in Britain in recent years, and about some key people in this development.

Lesson 6

You have learned to find out how religious people get on with each other in your local area, and held a meeting about it.

Lesson 5

You have learned how religious people have sometimes been in conflict but how many are working to achieve harmony as well.

UNIT 4: WHAT'S SO IMPORTANT ABOUT KEY RELIGIOUS FIGURES?

You will find out in ...

Lesson 1: What's so important about Abraham and Moses?

◎ Find out why the Torah is so important for Jews.

◎ Identify the covenants (agreements) made by God with Abraham and Moses and understand their importance.

◎ Think about the importance of keeping promises.

◎ Discuss and express ideas about the qualities that are important in someone we regard as a role model.

Lesson 2: What's so important about Jesus?

◎ Collect information that you already know about Jesus.

◎ Investigate how we know about Jesus and what Christians believe about him.

◎ Think about and explain your own beliefs about Jesus.

Lesson 3: What's so important about Muhammad?

◎ Find out how we know about Muhammad's life.

◎ Show knowledge and understanding of the important events in Muhammad's life and his important qualities as a religious leader.

◎ Think about the nature and consequences of life-changing experiences and show that you understand their importance.

Lesson 4: What's so important about Hindu teachers and scriptures?

◎ Understand why the teachings of the gurus needed to be written down.

◎ Find out about the different Hindu scriptures.

◎ Give your opinion on arguments for and against having so many scriptures.

◎ Interpret some extracts from the scriptures.

Lesson 5: What's so important about the Buddha?

◎ Think about the suffering in the world and the reasons for it.

◎ Find out how Siddhartha found enlightenment and write a diary entry to show knowledge and understanding of this.

◎ Express ideas about selfish desires in the modern world and how they can be overcome.

◎ Evaluate a meditation exercise.

Lesson 6: What's so important about Guru Nanak?

◎ Think about and discuss the skills needed by a good teacher, particularly a religious teacher.

◎ Create an item for a news programme or newspaper article to show knowledge and understanding of Guru Nanak's life-changing experience.

◎ Decide on the most important rule for living a good life and justify your choice.

What's so important about key religious figures?

1. What's so important about Abraham and Moses?

Think about the books you have. Do you have a favourite one, or one that is special to you? What makes it so special? Perhaps it was a gift, or you just love reading it.

Jewish people know about Abraham and Moses, two people who are very special to them who lived long ago, because of a very important book called the Torah. Abraham and Moses are also regarded as prophets by Muslims, to whom they are known as Ibrahim and Musa.

ACTIVITY ONE ....

Read the information section below. Try to work out why the Torah is special for Jews.

Have you ever wondered how we know things about people who lived a very long time ago? Over the centuries scholars have tried to find out as much as they can about people who lived thousands of years ago, but who are still regarded as really important today. At first, information about such people was passed on from one generation to another by word of mouth, but then it was written down.

ⓘ Why the Torah is special for Jews

Judaism began with two leaders, Abraham and Moses. Jews know about them because they can read about them in the first part of the Jewish scriptures, called the Torah. The word 'torah' means 'law'. Jews believe that Moses received the Torah from God and that it is the laws in the Torah that Jews need to obey to keep their relationship with God and with others. Jews think that the Torah is God's greatest gift; and that its words are God's words. The Ten Commandments are the most important of the laws.

▶ A Torah Scroll. It is sacred because it contains the laws God revealed to Moses. It is kept in a special cupboard in the synagogue called the Ark.

ⓘ What do we know about Abraham and Moses?

Abraham

Abraham was born about 4000 years ago. While people around him worshipped many gods, he only believed in one eternal (everlasting) god. God made an agreement with him that, if he went to a new land with his family and obeyed God in everything, he would become the father of a great nation. God and Abraham both kept their promises and Abraham became one of the **patriarchs** (father figures).

God's promise to Abraham

'Leave your country, your people and your father's household and go to the land I will show you. I will make you into a great nation and I will bless you; I will make your name great, and you will be a blessing.'

(From *Genesis 12:1-3*)

ACTIVITY TWO .....

A covenant means a promise or agreement. Jewish people believe that God made a promise to Abraham and Moses long ago that he is still keeping.

Write the promises made by God to Abraham and Moses in two speech bubbles. You must not use more than eight words in each bubble.

Moses

Hundreds of years later, the Jews had become slaves in Egypt. Moses, who is a descendant of Abraham, had a powerful religious experience when God spoke to him out of a burning bush. God told him he had been chosen to set the people free. Although he found it very hard, Moses obeyed God's instructions. After several plagues, Moses led his people out of Egypt (this was called the Exodus), across the Red Sea and back to Canaan, the 'Promised Land'. This event is remembered each year by Jews in the festival of **Pesach**. Although Moses died before reaching Canaan, God gave him the Torah on Mount Sinai on the way. God promised that the Jews would be his chosen people and that he would protect them. In return, the people must promise to keep God's laws. The Jewish festival of **Pentecost** celebrates the receiving of the law every year.

God's promise to Moses

*'"Now if you obey me fully and keep my **covenant**, then out of all nations you will be my treasured possession. Although the whole earth is mine, you will be for me … a holy nation."'*

(From *Exodus 19:5-7*)

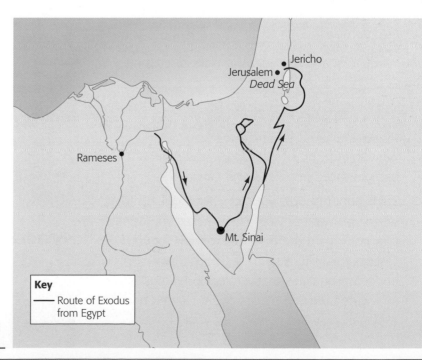

Key
— Route of Exodus from Egypt

▶ The route of Exodus from Egypt, including Mount Sinai

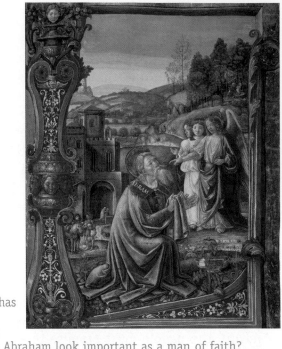

> How has the artist made Abraham look important as a man of faith?

> What moment in Moses' story is shown in this picture?

Do *you* think keeping promises is important?

ACTIVITY THREE ....

1. Write down a promise that you have made or might make to someone else in the near future.

2. Write down the consequences of keeping and not keeping the promise. Think about how the people involved might feel if you kept or broke the promise.

Be ready to share your ideas in class discussion.

ACTIVITY FOUR ....

1. Why do you think both Moses and Abraham have become popular Jewish figures?

2. Think about people you admire or look up to when you want advice. What makes you admire them or regard them as role models for you? Discuss this with a partner. Choose two important qualities that a role model must have and write them on pieces of card with a brief explanation of the reasons for your choices.

NOW TRY THIS ....

'It is never right to break a promise.' Write down why you agree or disagree with this statement.

KEY WORDS

Covenant a promise or agreement; also known as a 'testament'

Patriarch the male head of a family; a biblical person regarded as a key ancestor of the Jewish people

Pentecost a festival that celebrates the giving of the Jewish Torah to Moses

Pesach the festival of Passover, which celebrates the rescue of the Jews' ancestors, the Israelites, from slavery in Egypt. It is held in Spring each year

2. What's so important about Jesus?

Last lesson we looked at what and how we know about Abraham and Moses. We discovered that it is through the Torah that we know most about them. Now we are going to ask what and how we know about another important Jewish man, Jesus, who is believed by Christians to be not just a man, but the Son of God. Jesus is also regarded as a prophet by Muslims, to whom he is known as 'Isa.

ACTIVITY ONE ....

How do you imagine Jesus looked? Do a quick sketch. Ask yourselves how you know these things. After all, there are no photos!

ⓘ How do we know about Jesus?

Jesus lived from about 6BCE to about 30CE. Most of what Christians know about Jesus comes from his close friends and the Christian Church. The first writings about Jesus were letters written by his followers. Then accounts of Jesus' life and teachings were produced. These accounts led to the four **gospels**: Matthew, Mark, Luke and John. The first of these gospels dates from about 30 to 40 years after Jesus died. After a while all these writings were collected and put together to form the New Testament part of the Bible.

NOW TRY THIS ....

The gospels describe little about Jesus before he began his public work, and do not describe what he looked like at all. Why do you think this is?

Look at the pictures of Jesus here. They are all different because nobody knows what he looked like.

> A less traditional image of Jesus. What is the painter trying to tell us about Jesus?

> An icon of Jesus, an ancient painting that helps people worship Jesus

> A painting of Jesus by Holman Hunt. What is the light symbolising?

65

ⓘ What did Jesus teach?

Jesus taught people that God's Kingdom was coming, and evil and suffering would be overthrown. He taught that this would only happen if people truly loved their neighbours by caring for them, and loved God by keeping his commandments. He showed this teaching by performing miracles that gave back health and sanity to ill people. Although Jesus was a Jew, he upset the Jewish leaders of his time by his criticism of some of them, so they plotted his death. A large part of the gospels is about the last week of Jesus' life, when he was betrayed, tried and executed by crucifixion in Jerusalem in about 30CE.

ⓘ What did people believe about Jesus when he was alive?

*'He asked them [the **disciples**], "Who do people say I am?"*

'They replied, "Some say John the Baptist; others say Elijah*; and still others, one of the prophets."

'"But what about you?" he asked. "Who do you say I am?"

Peter answered, "You are the Christ."'

(From *Mark 8: 27-30*)

* Elijah was a Jewish prophet who was alive 800 years before Jesus

ⓘ What are the most important Christian beliefs about Jesus?

Christians believe that Jesus rose from the dead. Jesus' resurrection from the dead is the most important belief held by Christians because it means that evil, hatred and death are less powerful than good, love and life. Christians believe that those who follow Jesus will die, as he did, but will rise to new life, as he did. They believe that Jesus was not just a man, but was God himself in human form. They believe he was the Son of God, saving the human race from its own evil. Christians believe that Jesus was also the Jewish **Messiah** (Hebrew) or **Christ** (Greek)(both words mean 'the anointed one') whom the Jews expected to come one day and save people from their sins.

▶ A page of the gospels in Greek, written nearly 2000 years ago

ACTIVITY TWO ••••••••••••

1. With a partner, read the extract from the gospel written by Mark and try to identify the clues it contains about who Christians believe Jesus was.

2. Create a spider diagram to show five important Christian beliefs about Jesus based on the information.

3. Most Christians believe that the most important story about Jesus was his resurrection. Why do you think this is?

◀ What is happening in this picture? How is Jesus shown?

NOW TRY THIS

Many people think Jesus' teaching about the Kingdom of God has had a big effect on human society because his followers helped to start hospitals, schools, charities for the poor, etc. Others say that the world is as bad as it ever was, and point to continuing greed and violence. What do you think the effect of Jesus' teaching has been and is today?

ACTIVITY THREE ●●●●●●●●●●

1. Look at the list of words in the green box below. Divide them into two columns to show words that you think describe Jesus, and words that you don't think describe him, or you are unsure about.

Words that I think describe Jesus	Words that I don't think describe Jesus or that I am unsure about

2. Below the lists, try to explain why you think the words in your left-hand column describe Jesus and those in your right-hand column don't.

3. What evidence (proof) might you need to help you make up your mind about those you are not sure about?

> caring   idealistic   human   Messiah
> resurrected   crucified   good   stupid
> Saviour   foolish   brave   mad   prophet
> Christ   selfish   kind   a miracle worker
> Son of God

KEY WORDS

Christ	the Greek word for 'Messiah'; a title for Jesus used by Christians
Disciple	a learner or follower, usually of Jesus
Gospel	a word that means 'good news'. Some books in the New Testament are called gospels because they describe the good news Jesus taught
Messiah	a Hebrew word meaning 'anointed one'; the person the Jews expected to come to save them from their enemies
Peter	the leader of the first group of Jesus' disciples

3. What's so important about Muhammad?

SKILLS

• **finding out** about the life of Muhammad and the most important Muslim beliefs,
• **identifying** Muhammad's important qualities as a religious leader,
• **creating** a script to show understanding of his life,
• **thinking about** life-changing experiences and their consequences

ACTIVITY ONE ....

1. Some people have a motto in life such as 'Do as you would be done by' or 'Look after number one'. Do you have a motto? Does it describe how you try to live your life?

2. Look at the picture below. What are the two main beliefs declared in the Shahadah?

We have discovered that Jesus is important to Muslims as well as Christians, and that Muslims know him as the prophet 'Isa. Now we are going to ask what and how we know about the last and most important of the Muslim prophets, Muhammad.

A very important principle for Muslims is expressed in the Shahadah. It is the first of five requirements, known as 'pillars', that keep the Muslim faith strong, just as pillars hold up a building.

ⓘ What do we know about Muhammad?

Muslims have been able to learn about Muhammad in their holy book, which is called the Qur'an. They believe that Muhammad was Allah's final messenger or prophet, and that Allah's revelations to Muhammad are more important than all the others, including those to Ibrahim (Abraham), Musa (Moses) and 'Isa (Jesus).

▶ The Shahadah. The Arabic words mean, 'I bear witness that there is no God but Allah and that Muhammad is the messenger of Allah'.

Timeline: the life of Muhammad

Born in Makkah, now in Saudi Arabia. (His father had already died.)	His mother dies, so he goes to live with his grandfather and then an uncle.	He marries Khadijah, a widow and wealthy trader.
570CE	**576CE**	**601CE**

> The cave on Mount Hira where Muhammad received his first revelation. Why do you think Muhammed came here to meditate?

> The Qur'an

Muslims do not worship Muhammad because they do not believe that he was God. However, they believe that he was the last human used by God as a prophet and that all the words recorded in the Qur'an are God's direct words to Muhammad. Within twenty years of his death the Qur'an was completed, and has remained unchanged ever since. It is read in the original Arabic so that the meaning is not altered.

He has a life-changing experience. He is meditating in a cave at Hira when the Angel **Jibril** (Gabriel) appears to him and asks him to recite these words of God: 'Recite in the name of your Lord who created – created man from clots of blood. Recite! Your Lord is the Most Bountiful One, who by the pen taught man what he did not know.' (From *Sura 96.1-5, Qur'an*) Muhammad is filled with fear and doubt, but the angel comes again two years later. Throughout his life Muhammad could not read and write so he related the messages to his friends who memorised them and then wrote them down. The words became the Qur'an.	Some time after this Muhammad has another vision in which he is taken to Jerusalem on an animal like a horse with wings. From Jerusalem he is taken to heaven and speaks to earlier prophets. He is told that Muslims should pray five times a day. This night became known as the Laylat-ul-Qadr or Night of Power.	When Muhammad tries to proclaim (preach) he is ignored, laughed at and threatened, but he is determined to be heard so he and his followers flee to Madinah. Here people begin to accept his preaching and he builds his first mosque. The journey to Madinah became known as the Hijra, and Muslims count their calendar years from then, so 622CE is 1AH (Anno Hijra).	Muhammad dies after he returns to Makkah. He has continued to live simply and has preached that wealth should be shared with those in need. He has said that giving things up should be done out of great love for God.
610CE		**622CE**	**632CE**

ACTIVITY TWO ....

1. The three words below are adjectives that Muslims would use to describe Muhammad. Write three sentences about him, using one of these words in each. The dates above the adjectives give you a clue about what time in Muhammad's life your sentence should be about.

622CE	622CE	610CE
determined	brave	obedient

2. Muslims believe that it is disrespectful to draw pictures of Muhammad, so imagine you could have a conversation with Abu Bakr, a good friend of Muhammad, after Muhammad's death.

   Use the timeline to help you create five questions and answers about Muhammad's life. Your conversation could include the following information:

   - appearance of the Angel Jibril
   - Qur'an
   - praying
   - acceptance of Muhammad's preaching
   - effects on how people lived their lives
   - friendship of Muhammad and Abu Bakr (you'll have to use your imagination for this one).

Muhammad's first vision in the cave proved to be a life-changing experience for him.

ACTIVITY THREE ....

Create a cartoon strip made up of three pictures labelled 'Before', 'During' and 'After' about a life-changing experience that has happened to you or someone you know of.

NOW TRY THIS ....

Words from Muhammad's farewell sermon in 632CE

'All believers are brothers … You are not allowed to take things from another Muslim unless he gives it to you willingly. You are to look after your families with all your heart and be kind to the women God has entrusted to you. You have been left God's book, the Qur'an. If you hold fast to it, and do not let it go, you will not stray from the right path. People, reflect on my words. I leave behind me two things, the Qur'an and the example of my life. If you follow these you will not fail.'

(From *Hadith*)

In his last **sermon**, Muhammad gave his followers advice on how to live a good life. What advice on how to live a good life would you give to someone? Make sure you include at least one of Muhammad's pieces of advice. Explain your ideas.

KEY WORDS

Jibril	one of the angels of God who brought messages to Muhammad; known as Gabriel to Jews and Christians
Sermon	a talk given to worshippers on a religious topic by a leader

4. What's so important about Hindu teachers and scriptures?

SKILLS ↗

- **thinking about** why the teachings of the gurus needed to be written down,
- **finding out** about the different types of Hindu scriptures,
- **sorting** arguments for and against so many scriptures and working out your own views on this,
- **interpreting** some extracts from the scriptures ↘

Not every religion has a main person connected with its beginnings. Over the centuries, followers of Hinduism have been inspired by different gurus (teachers). It is believed that the Hindu scriptures reflect the ideas of these important figures.

ⓘ Hindu scriptures

There are many holy books in Hinduism. They can be divided into two categories – **smriti** and **shruti**. The shruti ('that which is heard') are thought to have been revealed to holy men directly from God in the very distant past. The most important are the **Vedas**, four books written in Sanskrit between 1500 and 800BCE. The most sacred is the Rig Veda, which includes over 1000 hymns and poems praising the gods. At the end of each Veda there are sections called the **Upanishads**. These record discussions between gurus and their followers about key beliefs, and were composed between 800 and 300BCE.

The smriti ('that which is remembered') are books based on what people could remember of God's message. They were written later, but include some of the best-loved scriptures about the gods and goddesses and famous heroes and villains. The most popular are two very long epic poems called the Mahabharata (which contains the Bhagavad Gita) and the Ramayana.

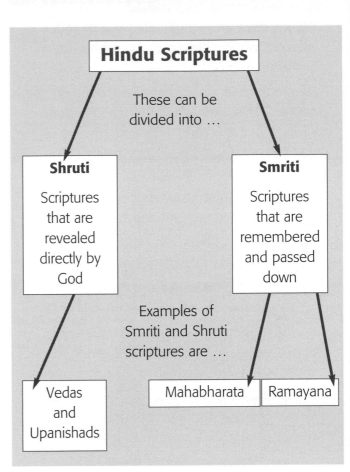

Hindu Scriptures

These can be divided into …

Shruti

Scriptures that are revealed directly by God

Smriti

Scriptures that are remembered and passed down

Examples of Smriti and Shruti scriptures are …

Vedas and Upanishads

Mahabharata | Ramayana

ACTIVITY ONE ....

1. Which do you think might be more important for Hindus, the smriti or the shruti holy books? Give a reason for your answer. Why might both be important?

2. Play a little game. Sometimes it is called 'Chinese Whispers'. Your teacher will whisper a message to the first person in the class. Still whispering, you all have to pass the message on to the next person until the last person repeats it to the teacher.

   How and why did the message change?

   Use this game, and any other ideas that you have, to discuss why it was necessary for the Hindu scriptures to be written down.

ACTIVITY TWO

1. Do you think it is a good thing that there are so many different scriptures and teachers in Hinduism, or not?

   Here are some possible answers to the question above. With a partner sort them into answers saying that it is a good thing and answers saying that it is not. Try to decide which side of the debate you would be on.

   a) It is very confusing when there are so many different scriptures and teachers.

   b) The variety of beliefs in Hinduism helps to make it a very tolerant religion.

   c) It helps to have so many different ideas because we do not all have the same way of thinking.

   d) The variety of beliefs makes it very hard for Hindus to be united in their message to the world.

   e) Nobody needs to feel left out in Hinduism.

   f) The differences between Hindus may lead to them disagreeing among themselves.

ⓘ Brhadaranyaka Upanishad

The Brhadaranyaka Upanishad compares the soul moving to the next life with a caterpillar:

'Now as the caterpillar, when it has come to the end of a blade of grass, in taking the next step, draws itself together towards it, just so this soul, in taking the next step, strikes down this body, dispels its ignorance, and draws itself together …'

ⓘ The Rig Veda and Vishnu

The Rig Veda describes the god **Vishnu** as the sky god who crosses the world in three steps:

'I will declare the mighty deeds of Vishnu, of him who measured out the earthly regions, Who propped up the highest place of the congregation; thrice setting down his footstep, widely striding. For this his mighty deed is Vishnu lauded [praised], like some wild beast, dread, prowling, mountain roaming; He within whose three wide-extended paces all living creatures have their habitation, Let the hymn lift itself as strength to Vishnu, the Bull far-striding, dwelling on the mountains; Him who alone with triple step hath measured this common dwelling-place, long, far extended.'

(From the *Rig Veda, 1:154*)

ACTIVITY THREE

1. Read the extract from the Rig Veda above. Draw an image of Vishnu based on the description in the extract.

2. Think of three adjectives that could be used to describe Vishnu, based on this extract, and include them in your drawing.

3. Read the short extract from the Upanishads on the left, which is about the soul preparing to move to its next life. With a partner try to think of as many alternative images as you can that could be used instead of the caterpillar. One example might be a snake shedding its skin.

▶ The Bhagavad Gita in Sanskrit and English

▶ Ramakrishna, a Hindu teacher of the 19th century who helped many people understand the teachings of Hinduism

NOW TRY THIS ....

Not all Hindu teaching is very old! The nineteenth-century guru, Ramakrishna, said this:

'There are pearls in the deep sea, but one must hazard (risk) all to find them. If diving once does not bring you pearls, you need not therefore conclude that the sea is without them. Dive and dive again. You are sure to be rewarded in the end. So it is with the finding of the Lord in this world. If your first attempt proves fruitless, do not lose heart. Persevere in your efforts. You are sure to realise him at last.'

Rewrite his teaching in your own words. Do you think he was right?

KEY WORDS

Smriti	'that which is remembered'; a term applied to some Hindu scriptures
Shruti	'that which is heard'; a term applied to the four Vedas, including the Upanishads
Upanishads	word meaning 'to sit down near'; groups of teachings added to the Vedas at a later date
Vedas	word meaning 'knowledge'; applied to the four oldest scriptures
Vishnu	Hindu God – the preserver

73

5. What's so important about the Buddha?

SKILLS

- **thinking about** and discussing why there is so much suffering in the world,
- **investigating** what Siddhartha did to find an answer to the problem of suffering and writing a diary entry to show your understanding of this,
- **expressing ideas** about craving in the modern world,
- **reflecting** quietly and then giving your opinion of doing this

ACTIVITY ONE ....

In groups, look at the first three examples of modern day versions of the types of suffering that Buddha saw. Are they the most serious examples of suffering do you think? If not, what would be more serious? Think to yourself whether you would be prepared to do anything about it.

One of the most famous people to come from India nearly 2500 years ago was the Buddha. He began life as a prince called Siddhartha Gautama, but his followers renamed him the Buddha when he discovered the meaning of life, which is called **enlightenment**. What and how do we know about him, and how did he come to be so famous?

The questions about suffering (**dukkha**) and what we can do about it troubled Siddhartha very much. One day he saw the fourth sight, a wandering holy man searching for the truth about life, and he decided to go and do the same!

The Four Sights

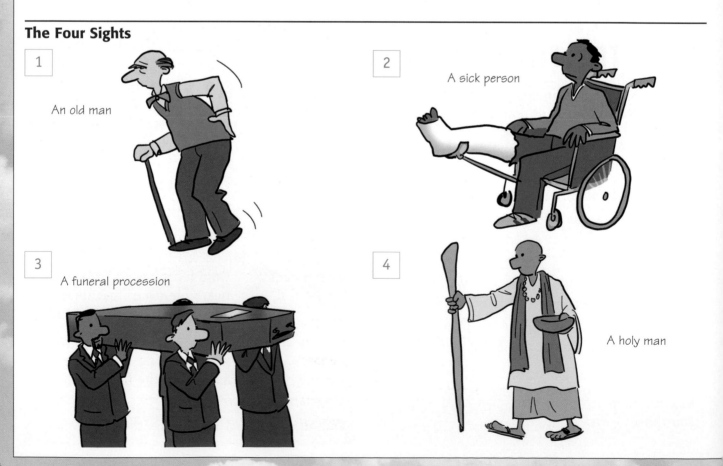

1 An old man

2 A sick person

3 A funeral procession

4 A holy man

A painting depicting the enlightenment of Buddha under a tree at Bodh Gaya. How has the artist shown that Buddha is an enlightened being?

ⓘ How Siddhartha found enlightenment

Siddhartha was 29 years old when he gave up his luxurious life in the palace to search for the truth and it was six years before he found answers that satisfied him. He spent some time listening to great teachers. Then he spent five years with five holy men, living a very hard life and eating and drinking as little as possible. In the end he found the answers to his questions by meditating (deep thinking) under a tree at a place called Bodh Gaya (look back to Unit 3, Lesson 2).

Buddhists say that Siddhartha became enlightened and so was called Buddha which means 'the enlightened one'. He became totally at peace with himself and the world around him. He was no longer filled with selfish desire and fear of suffering and death. Siddhartha then devoted the rest of his life to teaching others how to reach enlightenment or **Nirvana**.

Buddhists do not believe that Siddhartha Gautama was a god, but they believe that his teaching shows them the best way to live. While the Buddha was alive, his teachings (**dharma**) were not written down. After his death a special gathering of 500 monks met to repeat the teaching aloud. Monks passed the teaching by word of mouth for about 400 years until it was gradually written down.

ACTIVITY TWO ••••••••••••••

Read the information above to find out how Siddhartha eventually found the answers to his questions.

Imagine that you are Siddhartha. Write a diary entry for the day when you were enlightened. Include comments about how you felt as well as an account of what you were doing while searching for enlightenment. Say why you think people called you the 'Enlightened One' afterwards.

ⓘ Buddhacarita

The Buddhacarita, written in the second century CE, describes the moment when the Buddha reached enlightenment:

'The earth swayed like a woman drunk with wine, the sky shone bright with the Siddhas (men who have obtained perfection) who appeared in all directions, and the mighty drums of thunder resounded through the air. Pleasant breezes blew softly, rain fell from a cloudless sky, flowers and fruits dropped from the trees out of season in an effort, as it were, to show reverence for him.'

ACTIVITY THREE ••••••••••••

Look at the extract above about the Buddha's enlightenment. Write down three phrases that show that the moment when he reached enlightenment was a very special moment for the Buddha.

ACTIVITY FOUR ••••••••••••

In a sermon, the Buddha once said that suffering is caused by craving. With a partner:

1. Look up 'craving' in a dictionary and write the definition in the centre of a blank piece of paper. Write or draw around it as many examples of craving in the modern world as you can think of.

2. Choose one of your examples of craving to mime to the rest of the class, for them to guess what it is.

ACTIVITY FIVE ••••••••••••

The Buddha found his answer through meditation. This is something that some people learn to do over a period of time. A simple exercise to still your mind and meditate requires you to sit comfortably and quietly, close your eyes and breathe slowly and regularly. Then slowly tense and relax the various parts of your body. Concentrate on your breathing, in and out, slowly and quietly. Try it and say how it made you feel.

NOW TRY THIS ••••••••••

The Buddha suggested an eight-fold path to get rid of craving:

'And what is that middle path that gives us vision? Truly it is the noble eight-fold way, that is: right view, right aim, right speech, right action, right living, right effort, right mindfulness, right concentration.'

What do you think would work? Write down your ideas and explain them fully.

KEY WORDS

Dharma	teachings of the Buddha
Dukkha	suffering and everything unsatisfactory
Enlightenment	understanding the truth about the way things are
Nirvana	the state of perfect peace, free from selfish desires

6. What's so important about Guru Nanak?

The Sikh religion began when ten male gurus, starting with Guru Nanak, began to teach others what they believed.

ACTIVITY ONE

1. In small groups, make a list of the qualities you think are needed for someone to be a good school teacher.

2. Now think about religious teachers. What changes would you make to your list, if any?

Another famous person to come from India was Guru Nanak, although this was much later than the Buddha. What and how do we know about him, and how did he come to be so famous?

➤ Guru Nanak, the first of the ten gurus (left), and Guru Gobind Singh (above), the last of the ten gurus. The two gurus are portrayed very differently. What are the differences? Do they both appear to have the qualities of a good teacher, in your opinion?

ⓘ What do we know about Guru Nanak?

The first Guru was Guru Nanak. He was born in 1469 in the village of Talwandi, which is now in Pakistan. Although his family was Hindu, he was an accountant to a Muslim landlord. He gained a reputation for being especially devoted to God and exceptionally kind to others, even as a young man. The most famous story about Guru Nanak is about the time when he went to the river to bathe before his dawn prayers, and mysteriously disappeared. Three days later, when it had been assumed that he had drowned, he reappeared. He said that he had been in God's presence. Here is what happened according to Janamsakhi, which is a life story of Guru Nanak.

> 'The Almighty gave him a bowl of milk. "Nanak, drink the bowl," He commanded. "It is not milk as it may seem; this is nectar (**amrit**). It will give you power of prayer, love of worship, truth and contentment." Nanak drank the nectar, and was overcome. He made another bow, then the Almighty blessed him. "I release you from the cycle of birth, death and rebirth; he that sets his eyes on you with faith will be saved … Nanak, go back to the evil world and teach men and women to pray, give to charity and live cleanly."'

Guru Nanak had this experience when he was about 36 years old. He then devoted the rest of his life to God. He travelled and preached throughout India and set up the first Sikh community at Kartaur in the Punjab in about 1520. The word 'Sikh' comes from the word for 'someone who learns'.

The tenth and the last guru was called Guru Gobind Singh (see the picture on page 77). He said that after his own death the sacred scriptures should become the Guru, and so the Sikh holy book is now called the Guru Granth Sahib (see the photo to the right).

ACTIVITY TWO ....

EITHER

In groups prepare a news item, including an interview for an imaginary news programme about Guru Nanak's three-day disappearance. Your interview could be between Guru Nanak and the interviewer, or between the interviewer and one of the people out searching for Nanak.

OR

Create a newspaper article, including headlines and a picture, reporting on Guru Nanak's disappearance.

You should include information about the following in your news item:

- who Nanak was before his disappearance
- where he was when he disappeared
- who spoke to him
- what was said
- what Nanak was told to do after his disappearance.

GURU NANAK'S DISAPPEARANCE

▶ Guru Granth Sahib, the Sikh holy book. How is the book being treated in this photograph?

Guru Nanak believed that the way you lived was important for your religion. For him all people were equally important to God, whatever their religion. It was the way people live that really matters.

ACTIVITY THREE ....

With a partner, decide what you think is the most important rule for living a good life. Present it to the class and be ready to justify your choice.

KEY WORDS

Amrit   a liquid of water and nectar used by Sikhs to initiate new members of the Khalsa (brotherhood and sisterhood of Sikhs)

NOW TRY THIS ....

1. Guru Nanak emphasised in his teaching that people could find God in the way they lived their lives. One story says that one day he refused an invitation to dine with a rich man and chose instead to visit Lalo, a poor man. The rich man was angry, so Guru Nanak took some bread from Lalo's home to him. When he squeezed it, milk came out. When he squeezed the rich man's bread, blood came out. With a partner, try to work out the meaning of this story and write a modern-day version of it.

2. 'How you live is more important than what you believe.' Write a speech for a debate supporting or opposing this statement.

3. Use the diagram below to summarise what you have learned about three religious leaders. Put one thing you think is true of them all in the middle segment (3). In the segments linking two leaders (2) write one thing that they share, and in the outer segments (1) write what is true of that leader alone. They can be personal qualities or facts, for example, 'Had a life-changing experience.' Can you remember how many leaders that is true of?

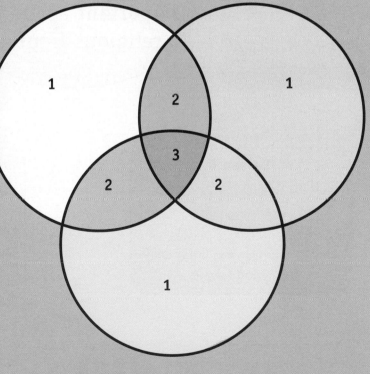

SUMMARY OF UNIT 4

Lesson 2
You have learned why Jesus is so important for Christians and other religious people, and how we know about him.

Lesson 3
You have learned why Muhammad is so important for Muslims and other religious people, as well as learning about the qualities of a religious leader.

Lesson 1
You have learned why Abraham and Moses are so important for Jews and other religious people, as well as learning about the importance of keeping promises.

What's so important about key religious figures?

Lesson 4
You have learned why Hindu teachers are so important for Hindus and other religious people, as well as learning about their scriptures.

Lesson 6
You have learned why Guru Nanak is so important for Sikhs and other religious people, as well as learning about the skills of a good teacher.

Lesson 5
You have learned why the Buddha is so important for Buddhists and other religious people, as well as learning about selfishness.

UNIT 5: WHAT SORT OF ATTITUDES RESULT FROM BEING RELIGIOUS?

You will find out in ...

Lesson 1: What attitudes do religious people have towards themselves?

◎ Think about how humans are treated differently to animals.

◎ Find out about religious attitudes to human beings.

◎ Compare the attitudes of the different religions.

◎ Express your own views about human beings.

Lesson 2: What attitudes do religious people have to life?

◎ Think about the purpose of life.

◎ Find out about religious attitudes to life and show your understanding of these.

◎ Express your own ideas about the purpose of your life.

Lesson 3: What attitudes do religious people have to God?

◎ Think about and discuss general attitudes to God.

◎ Find out what religious people think about God.

◎ Reflect on, talk about and explain your own ideas about God.

Lesson 4: What attitudes do religious people have to life after death?

◎ Think about attitudes to life after death.

◎ Find out about and show your understanding of religious ideas about life after death.

◎ Consider the kind of ceremony you would want people to hold after your death to reflect your own beliefs about life after death.

Lesson 5: What attitudes do religious people have to right and wrong?

◎ Think about situations when you have been treated unfairly.

◎ Find out about religious attitudes to right and wrong.

◎ Show your understanding of religious views.

◎ Reflect on, talk about and express your own ideas about what is right and wrong.

Lesson 6: What attitudes do religious people have to truth?

◎ Think about what we mean by truth.

◎ Find out what religious people think is true.

◎ Put religious views about truth into different categories.

◎ Reflect on and talk about your own ideas about what is true.

What sort of attitudes result from being religious?

1. What attitudes do religious people have towards themselves?

We have looked at what religion is about, and where it came from. We have also learned why some people are religious and in what different ways. Now we are going to look at the attitudes religious people have towards human beings.

ACTIVITY ONE ･･･････

'A dog is for life and not just for Christmas.'

What does this tell you about the way some people think about animals? Do we think of human beings in the same way? With a partner, make a list of five ways in which we treat human beings differently. Now, join with another pair and talk about why we do this. What conclusions have you reached?

ACTIVITY TWO ･･･････

Draw a human outline, to represent yourself, looking into a mirror. Use this drawing to describe your attitude to human beings. Put what you think of yourself inside the outline; put your attitude to other human beings outside the outline; and put the attitudes others might have towards you as a human being inside the mirror image.

What I think of others

What I think of myself

What I think others think of me

ACTIVITY THREE ············

Look at the information around the body below. It shows what different religions think about human beings.

Write a sentence about each of the following words to show either a similarity or a difference between two of the religions.

soul   God   body   human beings

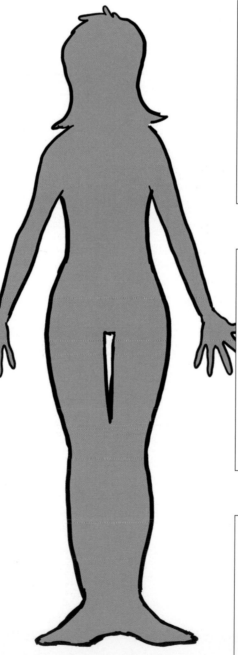

Judaism

Human beings are created by God 'in his image'. They are like God in some way. They have a higher importance than other creatures, but they are given responsibility for them. Humans have a soul that can return to God when they die.

Christianity

Human beings have a soul. If human beings decide to follow Jesus, whom God sent to be their saviour, their sins can be forgiven. They can become more like God, and will go to him when they die.

Islam

All human beings are created by Allah and are therefore equal. Humans are judged on how well they have lived. They are not like Allah but have been made from the earth. Each human has been given a unique soul. It is the soul that is the real person.

Hinduism

Every human being contains a divine spark, which is considered perfection. Depending on how good or bad a person has been in this life, the soul moves to a new body and a new life in this world after death.

Buddhism

This life is one of many. A person is made up of five ingredients (skandas): body, feelings, thoughts, ideals and awareness. These change from one life to another. Human beings, like the world and like life, are temporary. There is no real soul.

Sikhism

Men and women are equal. Everyone has a soul, which can move on to a new body after death, and can be freed from the circle of reincarnation.

NOW TRY THIS ....

1. Look at the following quotes. Which religions do you think they represent? What do they say about the attitudes of those religions towards human beings?

2. What do *you* think human beings are like? Do your views differ from the religious attitudes in question one?

QUOTE A: 'From the Lord's play all living creatures came, and from the Divine Light the whole creation sprang. Why then should we divide human creatures into high and low? The Lord, the Maker, has moulded one mass of clay into vessels of diverse shapes.'

(Guru Nanak)

QUOTE B: '…What is man that you are mindful of him the son of man that you care for him?

You made him a little lower than the heavenly beings and crowned him with glory and honour … You made him ruler over the works of your hands.'

(From Psalm 8: 4–7)

QUOTE C: 'Therefore, I urge you, brothers, in view of God's mercy, to offer your bodies as living sacrifices, holy and pleasing to God … be transformed by the renewing of your mind.'

(From Romans 12: 1–3)

QUOTE D: 'All have sinned and fallen short of the glory of God … But God shows his love for us in that while we were still sinners, Christ died for us. For as in Adam all die, so also in Christ shall all be made alive.'

(From Romans 5 and I Corinthians 15)

QUOTE E: 'You people! We have created you from a male and a female, and made you into nations and tribes, that you might get to know one another.'

(From Sura 49.13, Qur'an)

QUOTE F: 'Every soul is potentially divine. Devotion to God should be by identifying the self (soul) with Brahman. In this way race and caste are transcended.'

(Sadhu Atmasirarupdas)

QUOTE G: 'So God created man in his own image, in the image of God he created him; male and female he created them. God blessed them and said to them, "Be fruitful and increase in number, fill the earth and subdue it."'

(From Genesis 1.28–9)

2. What attitudes do religious people have to life?

SKILLS

• **thinking about** the purpose of your life,
• **looking at** religious beliefs about the purpose of life,
• **expressing** your own ideas about life's purpose

ACTIVITY ONE

Have you ever wondered why you were born? Not how you were born (you know that already!), but what is the purpose? Discuss this idea with a partner. What do you come up with?

We have looked at the attitudes religious people have towards themselves. But what attitudes do religious people have towards life itself?

The circle of life

▶ Jewish people believe that the purpose of life should be to develop the likeness of God in everyone. This means studying the Torah and living morally by following the duties such as 'honour your parents', 'do not kill' and 'do not steal'. Here a Jewish boy becomes Bar Mitzvah, a 'son of the commandment', and accepts this responsibility in life.

▶ Hindus believe that the purpose of life is a search for union with God, and to achieve **Moksha**. Moksha is the freedom from the cycle of birth and rebirth. They can achieve this by avoiding evil, fulfilling their religious duty and looking after their family.

▶ Buddhists believe that the purpose of life is to reach Nirvana. Nirvana is a state of peaceful nothingness. Some Buddhists seek this through meditation on the life and teachings of the Buddha. Some join a community of monks (called the **Sangha**), and some follow Buddhist practices in everyday life.

▶ For Christians the purpose of life is to love God and love one's neighbour. They can do this by following the way of Jesus. Baptism, as a child or an adult, is a sign that the old life has been washed away. Then, through God's influence (the Holy Spirit), the process of following Jesus' commandments to love one another begins.

▶ Humanists believe that birth is the beginning of life. Humans have to make the best of life by themselves, because they are made of only a body with a brain. Humanists believe that we have to make our own purpose for life while we are alive because there is no God or other world to give us any meaning. It is up to us! Then humans die. That is the end.

▶ Muslims believe that the purpose of life is to believe in and submit (give) themselves to Allah. They must not use their free will to disobey him. Life on Earth is a test of character. Here a newborn baby is being told that there is no God but Allah, and Muhammad is his prophet.

▶ Sikhs believe that the purpose of life is to travel on a spiritual journey, remember God, earn an honest living and share your earnings with people less fortunate than themselves.

ACTIVITY TWO ••

Read the statements on the opposite page, which show what religious and non-religious people think is the purpose of life, and then complete the following table:

According to ...	the purpose of life is ...
Jews	
Christians	
Muslims	
Hindus	
Buddhists	
Sikhs	
Humanists	

ACTIVITY THREE •••••••••••

1. Draw the outline of a tombstone.

2. The words that are sometimes put on people's tombstones are called **epitaphs**. Sometimes they are amusing, sometimes they are serious, depending on what that person or their family wanted to say. One example of a funny one is 'Here lies Fred, Who was alive, But now is dead.' Write a suitable epitaph for a person from one (or more) of the religions on this page. Use words and pictures to show the purpose of that person's life.

ACTIVITY FOUR •••••••••••••

1. Of all the beliefs written on the previous page, which do you think best fits with what you think the purpose of life is all about?

2. Draw another tombstone and add the epitaph that shows your purpose in life, and how you would like people to remember you.

NOW TRY THIS •••••••••••

Make a list of similarities and differences between religious and non-religious views on the purpose of life.

KEY WORDS

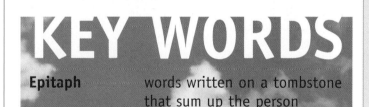

Epitaph	words written on a tombstone that sum up the person buried beneath it
Moksha	release from the cycle of being born and dying
Sangha	the brotherhood of Buddhist monks

3. What attitudes do religious people have to God?

SKILLS

- thinking about attitudes to God,
- finding out what religious people think about God,
- reflecting on, talking about and expressing your own ideas about God

We have looked at what religious people think about themselves and about life. What do they think about God?

ACTIVITY ONE

Opinion polls around the world suggest that about three-quarters of the world's population believe in God. Do a quick straw poll of your class and see if you get the same result. If not, why do you think that is? Discuss this with a partner.

You will quickly realise that you first need to ask the question, 'What do people mean by God?'

ACTIVITY TWO

Here are some people's views about God. Pick the three you most agree with and the three you least agree with. Why have you picked these? Discuss this with a partner.

1. *'I don't believe in God, but I'm very interested to meet her.'*

    (Arthur C. Clarke, science fiction writer)

2. *'He is God, the One, the Only; God the Eternal, the Absolute.'*

    (Surah 112, *Qur'an*)

3. *'There are 99 names that are God's alone.'*

    (Muhammad in *Hadith of Bukhari*)

4. *'Hear O Israel, the Lord our God is One.'*

    (Deuteronomy 6.1, *The Torah*)

5. *'If God made the world, who made God?'*

    (Martinne, aged 13)

6. *'The Lord is my shepherd; I shall not want.'*

    (Attributed to King David, *Psalm 23*)

7. *'There in One God, Eternal Truth, Creator of all things.'*

    (Ik Onkar, Mool Mantar, *Guru Granth Sahib*)

8. *'Call on God, but row away from the rocks.'*

    (Indian proverb)

9. *'It is the creative potential itself in human beings that is the image of God.'*

    (Mary Daly)

10. *'I know God will not give me anything I can't handle. I just wish he didn't trust me so much.'*

    (Mother Teresa)

Islam

'Say: "God is One, the Eternal God. He begot none, nor was he begotten. None is equal to him."'

(From *Sura* 112.1–4, *Qur'an*)

'Allah is the greatest; Allah is the greatest; Allah is the greatest; Allah is the greatest; I bear witness that there is no God but Allah.'

Judaism

'… I saw the Lord seated on a throne, high and exalted, and the train of his robe filled the temple. Above him were seraphs (glorious beings), each with six wings … And they were calling to one another: "Holy, holy, holy is the Lord Almighty; the whole earth is full of his glory."'

(From *Isaiah* 6.1–4)

Christianity

'And being found in appearance as a man, he humbled himself and became obedient to death — even death on a cross! Therefore God exalted him to the highest place and gave him the name that is above every name …'

(From *Philippians* 2.8–10)

Buddhism

► There is no personal God in Buddhism. The Buddha is not a god. He is a teacher of wisdom and goodness. Mahayana Buddhists believe that there are spiritual beings in the universe, including animals, gods and bodhisattvas (enlightened beings who return to help others rather than go to Nirvana). Images of these and Buddha are used as a focus for prayer and meditation but they are not worshipped.

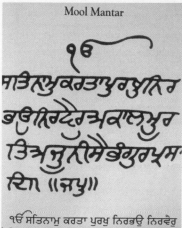

Sikhism

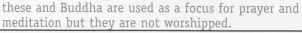

Mool Mantar

ੴ ਸਤਿਨਾਮੁ ਕਰਤਾ ਪੁਰਖੁ ਨਿਰਭਉ ਨਿਰਵੈਰੁ
Ik Onkaar Satnaam Kartaa Purakh Nirbhau Nirvair
ਅਕਾਲ ਮੂਰਤਿ ਅਜੂਨੀ ਸੈਭੰ ਗੁਰਪ੍ਰਸਾਦਿ॥
Akaal Moorat Ajooni Saibhang Gurprasaad.

'There is one God, Eternal truth, Creator of all things and the all-pervading spirit, fearless and without hatred, timeless and formless, beyond birth and death, self-enlightened, by the grace of Guru is God known.'

Hinduism

► Hindus believe that there is only one God, called Brahman. He is called by different names and can be worshipped in many forms. Brahman controls the universe through Brahma (the Creator), Vishnu (the Preserver) and Shiva (the Destroyer), but many other gods represent other forms of Brahman. Many Hindus also believe that the gods have come to earth in human or animal forms (avatars), such as Rama and Krishna, to help them.

ⓘ Information

Jews, Christians, Muslims and Sikhs all believe in one God who is the greatest. He is the cause of all things, and the source of all life. He is both near (immanent) and above all things (transcendent), fair and merciful, invisible and untouchable. Yet he is a God that people can relate to, for he hears prayers and protects and comforts people. He is active in historical events and works through special people.

ACTIVITY THREE ....

Look at the pictures on the previous page and the information above and find out what different religions think about God.

1. Read each of the statements below and, in groups, choose the religion or religions that agrees with each statement. The first is done for you.

   a) There is only one God. *Christianity, Judaism, Sikhism and Islam*.

   b) There is no personal God.

   c) God is the greatest being there is, and nothing else is like God.

   d) God shows himself in human forms.

   e) God can be worshipped in different forms.

   f) God is the creator of all things.

   You might be able to add other statements.

2. Discuss how easy you found this.

NOW TRY THIS ....

Look again at the information that describes what religious people think about God. How might you expect them to show this in what they actually do?

Using one or more of the following phrases, write three sentences to show how religious people show their attitudes about God.

worship   pray to   make images of   fear
honour   obey   laugh at   take seriously
please   love   respect   seek forgiveness from
ignore   befriend   feed   carry about   dress

ACTIVITY FOUR ....

One of the most difficult **philosophical** questions is what does God mean? God may mean different things to different people. Children may have a different idea of God from older people. What does the idea of God mean to you?

KEY WORDS

Philosophical   meaningful, understandable or logical

4. What attitudes do religious people have to life after death?

SKILLS

- **thinking about** attitudes to life after death,
- **finding out** about religious beliefs about life after death,
- **reflecting on, talking about** and **expressing** your own ideas about life after death,
- **using your imagination** to think ahead

Is there life after this life? This is an important question that human beings have always asked themselves. Have you ever wondered about this? Religious people have, and they have different attitudes to it.

Some religions believe that when somebody dies, their soul moves to another body to live another life. This is called reincarnation. Others think that people only live one life but are judged when they die. If they have been good, their soul is allowed into **heaven**, but if they have been bad, their soul is sent to **hell**. Others believe that when we die, that is it, and there is no after-life at all.

Have you ever had the feeling that you have done something or been somewhere before? This is called *'déjà vu'* (French for 'already seen'). Why do you think we get these feelings? Some people, who believe in reincarnation, say it is because we have lived a previous life and are now living another life. Other people say that believing in life after death is an escape from the fact that when we die we are finished for ever. Others say that if this is the only life there is, what is the point of it?

ACTIVITY ONE ....

What do you think about life after death?

Do you believe in reincarnation, or in the Day of Judgement, or that when we die that is it? Or do you think something else?

> An old cemetery. What does it make you feel?

91

Judaism

When the Jewish scriptures were written Jews believed that, after death, everyone went to Sheol - a dark place below the earth where people's spirits stayed for ever. Later on, Jews accepted the idea that there might be some kind of eternal life, in which people would be rewarded for good deeds or punished for wrongdoing.

'I believe with perfect faith that there will be a resurrection of the dead at a time when it will please the Creator, blessed be his name …'

(From *Principles of Faith,* *Maimonides*)

Christianity

Christians believe that when Jesus rose from the dead he overcame the power of death for ever. Those who believe in him therefore will also be resurrected to new life. At the end of all time and all things, Jesus will return as judge, and those who have lived according to his commands will be able to join God. Those who have not will be separated from God because that was their choice. This is what Christians mean by heaven and hell. Many years ago, these destinies were described by writers and painters as places of bliss and fire populated by angels or devils.

'I am the resurrection and the life. He who believes in me will live, though he die, and whoever lives and believes in me will never die.' (Jesus)

Islam

Muslims believe that, without belief in life after death, life on earth would be meaningless. On the Day of Judgement (**Akhirah**) good people will go to paradise and be with Allah, but bad people will go to hell.

'Those who have embraced the Faith and done good works will rejoice in a fair garden, but Those who have disbelieved and denied Our revelations and the life to come, shall be delivered up for punishment.'

(From *Sura 30.15–16, Qur'an*)

Sikhism

Sikhs believe that it is possible to find freedom in this life, but if this doesn't happen, the soul will be born again into another body to continue its path towards union with God. The soul cannot go backwards.

'Know the real purpose of being here, and gather up your treasure under the guidance of the true Guru. Make your mind God's home. If he abides in you undisturbed, you will not be reborn.'

(From *Kirtan Sohila,* an evening prayer)

Buddhism

Buddhists believe that this life is one of many, so many they cannot be counted. At death, our life passes to a new body just as the flame of a dying candle can light a new one. There is no soul, only a continuous process where one life leads to the next, until greed, ignorance and hatred have been removed. This leads to Nirvana, a peaceful state of nothing.

Hinduism

Hindus believe that when the body dies, it perishes, but the soul, which never dies, is released from it to assume a new body, depending on the actions of the previous life. The theory that we get what we deserve is called **karma**.

'As a man leaves an old garment and puts on one that is new, the spirit leaves his mortal body and branches on to one that is new … The spirit that is in all beings is immortal (will not die) in them all: for the death of what cannot die cease to sorrow.'

(From *Bhagavad Gita 2.22 and 30*)

Humanism

For humanists, there is no after-life. The present life is all there is, so to speak or think of another life is a waste of time.

'The life of man, solitary, poor, nasty, brutish and short.'

(Thomas Hobbes)

ACTIVITY TWO ....

Read the information on the opposite page. Then, go back to your answer in Activity One. Has what you thought about life after death changed, or not? Explain your answer.

ACTIVITY THREE ....

1. Draw two diagrams like this to represent the two different types of religious belief in an after-life. Look at the information on the left again and use it to help you decide which diagram you think should be titled 'reincarnation' and which should be titled 'Day of Judgement'. Write these over the diagrams.

2. Label your diagrams to show why these shapes have been chosen to represent those forms of belief. These words might help you:

   heaven hell rebirth continuous judgement day

3. Write a definition of reincarnation and Day of Judgement under the appropriate diagram.

4. Write the names of the religions that believe in each of the views of life after death underneath the diagrams.

NOW TRY THIS ....

What people believe about an after-life may affect how they live and behave in this life. For example, Muslims believe that in the next life bad people will go to hell. Therefore, in this life most Muslims try to do good things and not bad ones.

Write down two other examples of how belief in an after-life might affect the way people behave in this life. Here are some words that might help:

forgiveness   kindness   duty   belief
prayer   worship

ACTIVITY FOUR ....

People's ideas about an after-life often decide what kind of ceremony they want when they die. Think about your own views on an after-life. What kind of ceremony, if any, would you like people to arrange for you after you have died and why?

KEY WORDS

Akhirah	Muslim belief in the Day of Judgement
Heaven	where God is found to his full extent
Hell	where God is absent; separated from God
Karma	Hindu and Buddhist principle that determines the consequences of one life for another

5. What attitudes do religious people have to right and wrong?

SKILLS

- **thinking about** situations when you have been treated unfairly,
- **finding out** religious attitudes to right and wrong,
- **showing** your understanding of religious attitudes,
- **reflecting on, talking about** and **expressing** your ideas on what is right and wrong

Thinking about right and wrong is called **ethics**. Living and acting according to what you think is right and wrong is called **morality**. These words, ethics and morality, are often used to mean the same thing. How do religious people live according to how their religion regards right and wrong?

▶ The Statue of Justice. What do you think the scales mean?

ACTIVITY ONE ....

'That's not fair!' I bet you've said that once or twice! Think of some examples when you were not treated fairly and explain why you thought it was unfair.

The idea of some things being fair or unfair only works if we think that some things are right and good, and other things are wrong and bad. What religious people think about right and wrong influences their idea of **justice**, and the way they think they should behave.

ACTIVITY TWO ....

Read the following information about what religious people believe is right and wrong. Write down the names of the different sets of rules you find in each of the religions. One example is Judaism and The Ten Commandments.

ⓘ Information

Judaism

The story of Adam and Eve disobeying God by giving in to the temptation of Satan shows the Jewish belief that God gave human beings free will, but humans still have to choose to obey him or not. Human beings often make the wrong choice, and the consequence of that is suffering. Jews find guidelines for doing what is right in the Ten Commandments, which are to be found in the Torah. These require Jews to do their duty to God and to other people.

Hinduism

Dharma is a sense of duty, so living morally is an essential part of Hindu life. Your duty depends a lot on your occupation. The teachings of gurus help Hindus to know what is right as their circumstances in life change. The duty for each stage of life (ashrama) is carefully set out. The Laws of Manu, for example, talk about 'the student stage' and say:

'Let him not injure others in thought or deed; let him not utter speech that makes others afraid of him … Let him abstain from doing injury to loving creatures, … from desire, anger, greed … and lying.'

Many Hindu teachers have emphasised the importance of ahimsa. This means non-killing, or non-injury.

Christianity

Like Jews, Christians find guidelines for right and wrong in their scriptures. Christians also think that the death of Jesus releases people who believe in him from the power of evil. Jesus also taught the importance of forgiveness, for everyone has done bad things and can only be truly forgiven if they are willing to forgive others. Jesus also taught the importance of love. He summed up the whole of the Torah for his followers when he told them to love God and love their neighbours. Some of the most important guidelines for Christians are in the sayings known as the Beatitudes, for example:

'Happy are those who show mercy, for mercy will be shown to them. Happy are the peacemakers, for they shall be called the children of God.'

Islam

Like Jews and Christians, Muslims also believe that they find what is right and wrong set out in their scriptures. Muslims must be determined to follow the will of Allah as it is set out in the Qur'an and follow the example of Muhammad. It is wrong to drink alcohol or to take other drugs because it helps Shaytan or Iblis (Satan) to catch Muslims off-guard and lead them into temptation.

Sikhism

Sikhs believe they should serve God by teaching the truth and defending justice. Duties are symbolised by the Five Ks:

Kesh ('uncut hair') – dedication to God

Kanga ('comb') – cleanliness and discipline

Kirpan ('dagger') – ready to fight for justice and protect the weak

Kara ('steel bracelet') – oneness of God and bond between Sikhs

Kachera ('cotton shorts') – the need for modesty and purity

Earning a living by honest means is a duty to God. Pursuing money for its own sake was said to be a bad thing by Guru Nanak. Sharing your wealth with others was a good thing.

Buddhism

The way that Buddhists should live is written in their scriptures, and is as follows:

To refrain from (keep from) taking life

To refrain from taking that which is not given

To refrain from sexual misconduct

To refrain from telling lies

To refrain from taking any kind of drug

These are called the Five **Precepts**.

Buddhists who live in a sangha have more rules.

ACTIVITY THREE ●●●●●●●●●●●

1. Draw two overlapping circles like the ones shown here. Label one circle 'good/right' and the other 'bad/wrong'. Read the information again and put into the circles what the religions believe is good/right and bad/wrong. An example for each circle is honesty and theft.

2. Where the circles overlap, write things that could be used in either a good or bad way, or which might be either right or wrong, depending on how they are used. An example might be money.

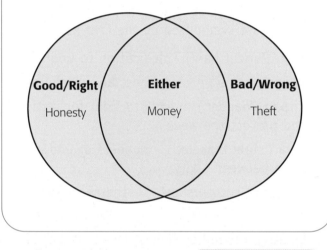

Good/Right — Honesty
Either — Money
Bad/Wrong — Theft

NOW TRY THIS ●●●●●●●●●●●

Even when people believe that they should do the right thing, working out what the right thing actually is may not be easy. They may disagree. Think of a situation where it is hard to work out what is the most loving thing to do. For example, punishing a murderer.

a) What different attitudes might people think are right?

b) Where might religious people get guidance on this?

Where do you get your ideas of right and wrong from? If they come from your family or upbringing, where did your family get them from?

ACTIVITY FOUR ●●●●●●●●●●●

Here are three real-life examples where people today have to decide what is right and wrong:

• experiments on animals,

• building more houses,

• carrying identity cards.

a) What would you decide for these situations?

b) What makes you think you are right?

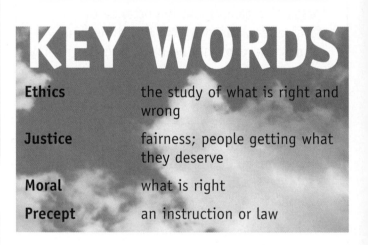

KEY WORDS

Ethics	the study of what is right and wrong
Justice	fairness; people getting what they deserve
Moral	what is right
Precept	an instruction or law

6. What attitudes do religious people have to truth?

SKILLS

• **thinking about** what we mean by truth,
• **finding out** what religious people think is true,
• **reflecting on** and **talking about** your ideas of the truth, putting religious ideas about truth into different categories

Religious people do not all believe the same things, so how can they know what is actually true?

Searching for the truth has been compared to climbing a misty mountain with many paths to the top. Why do you think that is?

ACTIVITY ONE ....

1. Look at the pictures of the car below. Which do you think is the truest picture or best representation of it?

2. In what way might they all be true or all be false? What does this tell you about truth?

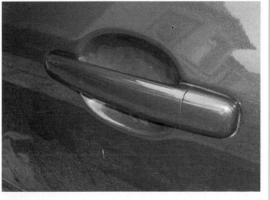

Knowing what is true is easy for some things but not for others. Being true is not the same as being proven to be true. People can disagree about the **truth**. Sometimes two people might both be right if they look at things from different angles.

ACTIVITY TWO

Read the banners here, which show three different theories about the truth of religions. All three theories can be held by different people within different religions.

1. Draw three banners of your own. Inside each write a slogan to illustrate what a follower of a religion would say about it if they held an exclusivist or inclusivist view of their religion. For example, a slogan for pluralism might be, 'Different ways but the same journey'.

2. Discuss with your partner how you think people of other religions would feel about your slogans.

3. Look at the picture of the mountain on the previous page. How does this illustrate a way of looking at the truth of religions?

Exclusivism – the **theory** that only one religion is right (that is, it *excludes* the possibility of truth in others).

Inclusivism – the theory that the truth of one religion is to be found in others as well (that is, *included* in the truth of another religion).

Pluralism – the theory that there is a plurality of (many) religions and they are all true for those who believe them.

All the religions believe that there is truth in their holy books, but sometimes, different people within religions have different ideas about how that truth can be found and understood.

KEY WORDS

Theory a hypothesis or view, based on evidence, that has yet to be proved to be true

Truth the way things really are; what is correct, right and actual

ACTIVITY THREE

Think about this. A person might be a mother, a daughter, a sister and a friend. Is it true that she can be all of these different things at the same time? Are you like this as well? Draw a circle with your name in it, and on the outside write down all the different people you are to others. What does this illustration tell you about the way in which truth may be viewed in religions?

ⓘ Information

Judaism

For Jews, the truth lies in their scriptures and is reflected in their special relationship with God. Jewish tradition claims that the scriptures contain the truth because they were given directly to Moses by God and contain God's words. Other Jewish books such as the Talmud have been written to help the Jewish people interpret what is in the Torah. Some Jews, who are called progressive, have argued that the Torah must be interpreted according to modern times.

Christianity

Christians believe that the Bible contains the truth about God and the world. Some Christians believe that every word in the Bible is literally true because the words have come from God, and so must be taken as they are. Other Christians believe that the Bible is the word (truth) of God but that the stories and events in it are often symbolic, and their meanings need to be interpreted for modern times.

Islam

Muslims believe that the Qur'an contains the truth because it is the direct words of God revealed to Muhammad by the Angel Jibril. The last verse he received was 'This day I have perfected your religion for you.' (*Surah 5:4, Qur'an*) The truth in the Qur'an is regarded as unchanging, unchangeable and untranslatable: 'O People, no prophet or messenger will come after me and no new faith will emerge.' (*Muhammad's Last Sermon*)

Hinduism

Hindus regard the Vedas, Upanishads, Bhagavad Gita and other scriptures as holy books but they are not regarded as the word of God. Only Brahman, with whom Hindus seek to be united, is truth. Brahman is found in all people and things. Gandhi based his policy of non-violent action on the principle of Satyagapha or 'truth force'.

Buddhism

Although the Buddha is greatly respected, Buddhists believe that people must find and experience the truth for themselves. The Buddha taught four noble truths about life as suffering, craving as the cause of suffering, the way to remove suffering and the path to follow. These are part of the Buddhist dharma, a word that also means 'truth'.

Sikhism

The highest authority is God. His truth is revealed through the Guru Granth Sahib. The Guru Granth Sahib is therefore highly revered and rests, covered with a cloth, on a cushion under a canopy, and is looked after almost like a person.

Baha'i

Baha'is believe that all religions are true in their own way and in their own time because they teach a truth about God in ways that made sense to people in different times and places. They therefore believe that all religions have some truth within them.

NOW TRY THIS ....

Read the information on this page. Draw one (or more) pictures of the holy books that are mentioned here. Draw it lying open, and write a label giving its name. Underneath each drawing write out the attitudes to the truth contained in the holy book by the followers of that religion.

SUMMARY OF UNIT 5

Lesson 2

You have learned that religious people have particular attitudes to life because of what they believe about the purpose of being alive as human beings.

Lesson 3

You have learned that religious people have some similar and different attitudes to God because of what they believe God is.

Lesson 1

You have learned that religious people have particular attitudes to themselves based on what they believe about being human.

What sort of attitudes result from being religious?

Lesson 4

You have learned that religious people have particular attitudes to life after death based on what their religion teaches about life and what happens, if anything, beyond it.

Lesson 6

You have learned that religious people have particular attitudes to what they think about the truth of different religions and their scriptures.

Lesson 5

You have learned that religious people have particular attitudes to right and wrong based on what their religion teaches about ethics and morality.

UNIT 6: SO WHAT DOES BEING RELIGIOUS MEAN?

You will find out in ...

Lesson 1: What does it mean to be religious? An investigation.

◎ Find out how to conduct an investigation.

◎ Consider the most important things to investigate.

◎ Plan your investigation.

◎ Talk about and express your ideas about this.

Lesson 2: What do case studies tell us about being religious?

◎ Find out, and reflect on, what it means to be religious.

◎ Decide what you think is most important about being religious and why.

◎ Apply what you have learned to real-life situations.

◎ Apply what you have learned to yourself.

Lesson 3: How can we present what it means to be religious?

◎ Work out what you know about being religious.

◎ Think about how to present what you know.

◎ Reflect on how best to communicate this to others.

◎ Communicate your knowledge and understanding using *PowerPoint® presentation graphics programme*.

Lesson 4: Guess who's coming to dinner!

◎ Think about what you have learned about religious leaders and religious figures.

◎ Reflect on what religious leaders and figures have in common and how they may differ.

◎ Decide what is most important about being religious in different religions.

◎ Work out how disagreements may be handled.

◎ Apply what you have learned to yourself.

Lesson 5: What can religious texts tell us about being religious?

◎ Think about what you have learned about being religious.

◎ Work out how these ideas are shown in religious texts.

◎ Interpret the texts.

◎ Apply what you have learned to yourself.

Lesson 6: So what does it mean to be religious? A debate.

◎ Find out about debates and how to take part in one.

◎ Decide on what you think about various aspects of religion and whether you would argue for or against them in a debate.

◎ Express your own ideas about what it means to be religious by taking part in a debate.

So what does being religious mean?

1. What does it mean to be religious? An investigation.

SKILLS

- **thinking about** what you have learned,
- **finding out** how to conduct an investigation,
- **reflecting on** the most important things to investigate,
- **talking about** and expressing your ideas,
- **planning** an investigation

We have looked at what religion is about, and where it came from. We have also learned why some people are religious and in what different ways. This unit brings your previous work together through an investigation of what it means for a person to be religious.

This means finding out what a religious person does, believes and wants in life, and how a religious person gets on with others.

ACTIVITY ONE ......

Decide which religion or religions you are going to investigate. You may choose from Judaism, Christianity, Islam, Hinduism, Buddhism, Sikhism or another religion. If you choose one religion, say Christianity, then the title of your investigation will be 'What does it mean to be a Christian today?' If you cover more than one religion, then the title will be 'What does it mean to be religious today?' You might want to contrast two ways of being religious in this case.

ACTIVITY TWO ....

Decide how you are going to present the findings of your investigation. You could prepare:

- a written research project with illustrations, statistics and diagrams
- a brochure or leaflet that might be used to inform others about what it means for a person to be religious
- a short textbook for younger children to explain to them what you have found out
- a poster
- a script for a TV or radio show
- a series of lessons for those who have not studied that religion
- an assembly presentation.

ACTIVITY THREE ••

Decide on the process of carrying out your investigation. What are you going to do first, second and third, for example? How long will you allow for these stages? When do you need to finish it by?

Your investigation may need to consist of:

- a case study of a member of each religion you are investigating (see Lesson 2: Activity One)
- a PowerPoint slide about the beliefs of each religion investigated (see Lesson 3: Activity One)
- a list of the similarities between the two religions you have chosen to investigate (see Lesson 4: Activities One, Two, Three and Four)
- examples and explanations of religious texts for your chosen religion or religions (Lesson 5: Activities Two and Three).

Fill in this information on a plan like the one below:

Title	What does it mean to be religious today?
Religion(s) to be investigated	Christianity and Islam
Presentation method	Leaflet
Method of investigation	Notes from my book
	Internet sites (www.bbc.co.uk/religion)
	My own experience
	Questioning family members and friends
Outline of project	
• Task 1	Introduction (main facts about my chosen religion(s) like name of leader; where the religion started)
• Task 2	A case study (a week in the life of a member of my chosen faith(s))
• Task 3	A factfile (interesting facts I find out)
• Task 4	Dinner table with guests and what they should talk about
• Task 5	Examples of religious aspects (belief; ritual; ethics; stories; experiences; social groups; buildings and objects)
• Task 6	Conclusion (summary of what I have found out)

The work you will be doing over the next few weeks will provide the basis of your investigation, but you might want to use other means of investigation, such as:

- interviewing, directly or by e-mail, religious people
- field-work at places of religion
- researching religions in books or on the internet.

You will have to think about where and when you might find information. Examples include:

- school and public libraries
- places of religious worship
- good internet websites
- people you know or can find out about
- class or home times.

ACTIVITY FOUR ••••••••••••

When you have completed your preparations, carry out your investigation.

NOW TRY THIS ••••••••••••

When you have come to the end of your investigation and have prepared the findings, think about what you have learned in the process. Ask yourself these questions:

1. Did the end product turn out as you had hoped at the beginning? If so, why was it so successful? If not, what happened to prevent it from turning out that way?

2. What were the easiest and what were the hardest things you had to do and why?

3. What new things did you learn during the investigation? How did you learn these things?

4. What things surprised you as a result of your investigation? Why was that?

5. How would you change your investigation if you had the chance to do it again?

6. What did other people think of your investigation when it was finished?

2. What do case studies tell us about being religious?

SKILLS

- **thinking about** what you have learned,
- **finding out** and reflecting on what it means to be religious,
- **deciding** what you think is most important about being religious and why,
- **applying** what you have learned to real-life situations,
- **applying** what you have learned to yourself

NOW TRY THIS ....

Change or add to the case studies to make it clearer that the person is very religious or takes religion very seriously. What changes did you make and why?

ACTIVITY TWO ....

1. Prepare a religious profile for yourself.
2. What have you learned about yourself?

We have looked at what religion is about, and where it came from. We have also learned why some people are religious and in what different ways. This unit brings your previous work together using some case studies.

ACTIVITY ONE ...... •

1. Read one or more of the case studies on the next two pages.
2. For each case study you look at, complete a religious profile, like the one below. You will not find all the information you need, but there are lots of clues that you can follow up by looking back at information in earlier units!

Name of person	Ravinder
Religion	Sikh
Beliefs they have	One God
Name of a religious leader they follow	Guru Nanak
Rituals they practise	Wearing a turban
Books they read	Guru Granth Sahib
What they think is right	Sharing their wealth
Experiences they have	Working in langar. Meeting to discuss charity work
Place of worship they attend	Gurdwara
Religious activities they do	Pilgrimage to Amritsar and the Golden Temple
Objects they use	Five K's

Also try to say how seriously religious you think the person is.

I think Ravinder is quite serious because he volunteers his time at the gurdwara to do charity work and help in the langar.

Name: Mandy

Occupation: Student

Weekday routine: Gets up, takes bus to university, eats ham sandwich for lunch, comes home, has dinner with family, does some study, meets friends in pub, watches documentary on animal cruelty, goes to bed.

Saturday routine: Gets up, goes shopping, eats veggie burger for lunch, goes to football match, returns home to change, goes to pub and on to club.

Sunday routine: Gets up very late after family have got back from Church, has lunch, does some study, watches 'Songs of Praise' on TV, has supper, goes to bed and reads the latest Harry Potter book.

Name: David

Occupation: Schoolboy

Weekday routine: Gets up, has breakfast, takes bus to school, eats beef sandwich for lunch, comes home. Mon-Thurs: has dinner with family, does some homework, attends Bar Mitzvah classes, helps mother with shopping at kosher butchers, goes to bed; Fri: dresses smartly and wears his kippah (skull cap) for special meal with family on this holy day called the Sabbath, doesn't watch TV, goes to bed early.

Saturday routine: Gets up, goes to synagogue and listens to readings about God from the Torah, has lunch, reads at home, has special meal with family, watches TV, goes to bed.

Sunday routine: Gets up late, eats roast lamb for lunch, does some study, watches TV, has supper, goes to bed.

Name: Zaki

Occupation: Bus driver

Weekday routine: Gets up early and prays to Allah, goes to bus garage and takes his prayer mat to use at prayer times in his breaks (prays five times a day), drives bus all day, eats sandwich for lunch, comes home, has dinner with family, prays and meets friends in local mosque and community centre and experiences feelings of brotherhood amongst members of faith, prays, goes to bed.

Saturday routine: Same as on weekdays but goes shopping for halal food.

Sunday routine: Gets up late after going back to bed after prayers, has lunch, relaxes around the house but fits in prayers with the family, reads Qur'an, cleans car, watches TV, has supper, goes to bed.

Name: Emma

Occupation: Student

Weekday routine: Gets up, has breakfast, gets dressed and puts on crucifix, takes bus to college, eats chicken sandwich for lunch, comes home, has dinner with family, does some study, meets friends in a café, watches programme about justice in Iraq, goes to bed.

Saturday routine: Gets up, goes shopping, eats hamburger for lunch, does some kind of exercise, returns home to change, goes to see friends.

Sunday routine: Gets up, goes to Mass, eats roast pork for lunch, does some study, watches TV, has supper, reads Bible and prays to God before going to bed.watches TV, has supper, reads Bible before going to bed.

Name: Ashok

Occupation: Waiter

Monday routine: Gets up, meditates, goes shopping, has lunch, relaxes around house, has dinner, goes to temple, volunteers at community centre to talk about dangers of drug use, returns home, reads and watches TV, goes to bed.

Tues–Sun routine: Gets up, meditates in front of statue of Buddha, has lunch, goes shopping, has early dinner, goes to work in restaurant, comes home late, goes to bed.

Name: Meena

Occupation: Housewife and part-time factory worker

Weekday routine: Gets up, worships one of many gods at shrine at home, organises breakfast for the children, does housework, has vegetarian lunch, goes to work at factory, comes home and prepares dinner with family, reads the children the story of Rama and Sita, goes to bed.

Saturday routine: Gets up, worships at shrine, goes shopping (signs anti-foxhunting petition), goes to mandir to help prepare lunch, stays for meeting with friends, comes home, watches TV, goes to bed.

Sunday routine: Same as on Saturday.

Name: Ravinder

Occupation: Teacher

Weekday routine: Gets up and dresses with his turban, has breakfast, goes to school, has vegetarian lunch, comes home, has dinner with family, does some marking, watches documentary on animal cruelty, goes to bed.

Saturday routine: Gets up, goes to gurdwara and listens to readings from Guru Granth Sahib, works in langar (dining-room in the gurdwara), returns home, watches TV, goes to bed.

Sunday routine: Gets up late, has lunch, prepares lessons for next week, goes to gurdwara for meeting about charity work, works on plans to visit Golden Temple at Amritsar, watches TV, has supper, goes to bed.

3. How can we present what it means to be religious?

SKILLS

- **working out** what you know,
- **thinking about** how to present what you know,
- **reflecting on** how to communicate it to others,
- **communicating** your ideas using PowerPoint

A PowerPoint presentation

We have looked at what religion is about, and where it came from. We have also learned why some people are religious and in what different ways. This unit brings your previous work together using a PowerPoint presentation.

To gather information about the different religions, you could look at the following pages:

- Buddhism: Unit 3: Lesson 2 (page 45) and Unit 4: Lesson 5 (page 74)
- Christianity: Unit 3: Lesson 1 (page 42) and Unit 4: Lesson 2 (page 65)
- Hinduism: Unit 3: Lesson 2 (page 45) and Unit 4: Lesson 4 (page 71)
- Humanism: Unit 3: Lesson 4 (page 51)
- Islam: Unit 3: Lesson 1 (page 42) and Unit 4: Lesson 3 (page 68)
- Judaism: Unit 3: Lesson 1 (page 42) and Unit 4: Lesson 1 (page 62)
- Sikhism: Unit 3: Lesson 2 (page 45) and Unit 4: Lesson 6 (page 77)

Unit 5 is very useful for finding out about the different beliefs about being human (see Lesson 1, page 82), life (see Lesson 2, page 85), God (see Lesson 3, page 88), life after death (see Lesson 4, page 90), right and wrong (see Lesson 5, page 94) and truth (see Lesson 6, page 97).

ACTIVITY ONE ··

Design a PowerPoint presentation to describe what you have learned about one or more of the following so far:

Buddhism   Christianity   Hinduism   Humanism   Islam   Judaism   Sikhism

On the next two pages are examples of PowerPoint presentations with slides to show how you might present your own. The information in these examples will also give you some ideas for the content of your slides.

ACTIVITY TWO ···············

Prepare just one PowerPoint slide that really describes you. What would you put on it?

NOW TRY THIS ············

Prepare a PowerPoint presentation to describe what you have learned about the way the religions of the world get on with each other.

Buddhism: my investigation

I have chosen three aspects of Buddhism

- Buildings
- Experiences

Explain why you have chosen these

You might like to add a third aspect, like stories.

Here are my findings about them

Buddhist Buildings

Buddhists worship in temples. The most important part of the temple is the shrine room.

Why is this the most important part? Add a reason.

I visited a Buddhist temple on my holiday in Thailand and here is a photograph of it

Experiences

Buddhists meditate to find a sense of peace. You could follow these instructions to experience meditating yourself.

Instructions

1. Sit or kneel still and comfortably
2. Slow your breathing to a regular relaxed pace
3. In turn, tense your muscles then relax them

Can you find another word for meditate to help explain its meaning?

Some other aspects of religion that you could use are:

- Beliefs (for example, in One God, Allah)
- Stories (for example, Rama and Sita)
- Ethics (for example, the Five Precepts)
- Rituals (for example, a Bar Mitzvah)
- Experiences (for example, a sense of peace during meditation)
- Social aspects (for example, sharing food in the langar at the gurdwara)
- Material aspects like buildings (for example, St Paul's Cathedral)

What does the word religion mean?

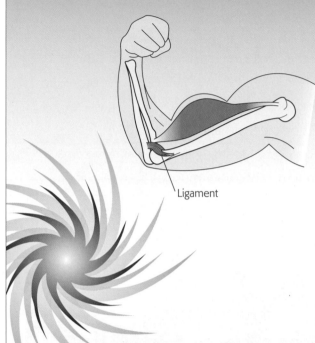

Ligament

Religion and ligament are similar. They both have **lig** in them.

A **lig**ament connects bones and muscles. It holds limbs together and enables them to move.

This shows what re**lig**ion is about because it also helps to keep people together and function as human beings.

Some ultimate questions

- Did the universe develop by chance?
- Why are we here?
- Is there a god?
- How do we know what is right and wrong?
- Why is there suffering?
- What happens when we die?

Religion helps people to answer these questions!

4. Guess who's coming to dinner!

SKILLS

- **thinking about** what you have learned about religious leaders,
- **reflecting on** what religious leaders have in common and how they may differ,
- **deciding what** you think is most important about being religious in different religions and why,
- **working out** how disagreements may be handled,
- **applying** what you have learned to yourself

We have looked at what religion is about, and where it came from. We have also learned why some people are religious and in what different ways. This unit brings your previous work together using an imaginary dinner.

ACTIVITY ONE

Draw a circle to represent a table, and put three small squares at equal distances from each other around the edge to represent chairs.

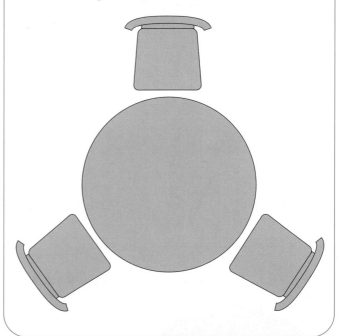

▶ People having a meal together. What would you talk about at your dinner?

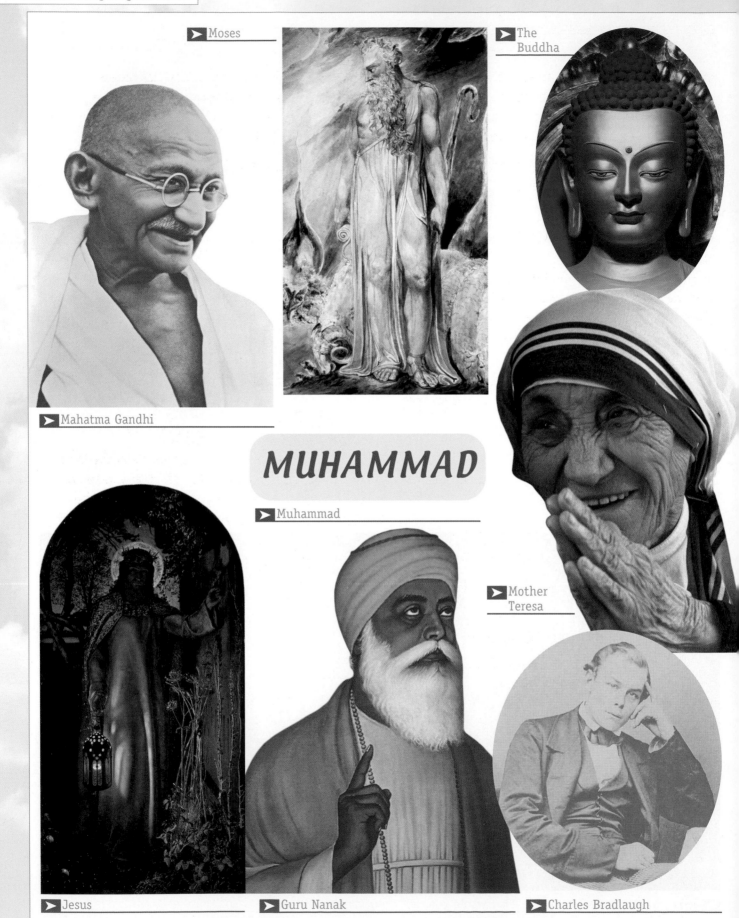

▶ Moses

▶ The Buddha

▶ Mahatma Gandhi

MUHAMMAD

▶ Muhammad

▶ Mother Teresa

▶ Jesus

▶ Guru Nanak

▶ Charles Bradlaugh

ACTIVITY TWO ....

Imagine you have invited three of the people pictured here to dinner. You are the waiter or waitress. Label the chairs in your diagram with the names of the three guests you have chosen.

This activity can be done more than once, with different combinations of guests.

ACTIVITY THREE ....

In groups of three use the information that comes earlier in this book or your work from last lesson to each find out about one of the personalities you have chosen. You can use the table below to help you. Concentrate on key events in their life, their important beliefs and their teachings to others. Be ready to feed back your information to the rest of the class.

Name of personality	Jesus
Events in life	Crucified for standing up for his beliefs
Beliefs	Believed in loving all people
Teachings	Taught about God's Kingdom

You can find particularly useful information on the following pages:

- Gandhi: Unit 3: Lesson 5 (page 54)
- Moses: Unit 4: Lesson 1 (page 62)
- The Buddha: Unit 4: Lesson 5 (page 74)
- Jesus: Unit 4: Lesson 2 (page 65)
- Muhammad: Unit 4: Lesson 3 (page 68)
- Guru Nanak: Unit 4: Lesson 6 (page 77)
- Mother Teresa: Unit 3: Lesson 1 (page 44)
- Charles Bradlaugh: Unit 3: Lesson 4 (page 51)

ACTIVITY FOUR ....

Look at the information you have gathered on your chosen guests and highlight on your tables the things they have in common, for example the things they all believe.

Write this information in the spaces between the guests.

NOW TRY THIS ....

Write down the topics that your chosen guests might disagree about on the table in your diagram. Try to suggest a way in which they might try to come to an agreement about one or more of these things.

ACTIVITY FIVE ....

If you were invited to join your guests at the table where would you choose to sit? Draw yourself on your diagram. Explain to your partners or to the class why you chose to seat yourself at that place.

5. What can religious texts tell us about being religious?

SKILLS

- **finding out** and reflecting on what you have learned about being religious,
- **working out** how a text contains or illustrates ideas, interpreting texts,
- **applying** what you have learned to yourself

We have looked at what religion is about, and where it came from. We have also learned why some people are religious and in what different ways. This unit brings your previous work together using some **texts**.

On this page and the next page are extracts from the writings of several religions and beliefs. These contain the teachings of these religions and beliefs, and so became very important and authoritative.

ACTIVITY ONE ·················

Read one or more of the extracts on these pages.

1. For each text, say which religion it is linked with. For example, The Qualities of Nirvana is linked with Buddhism.

2. Write out the main religious words in the text, and explain their meaning. Say why you think each is a religious word if you can.

   For example: Pray – to ask a question to a god. It is a religious word because of the connection with a god.

The Qualities of Nirvana

'Nirvana shares one quality with the lotus flower, two with water. As the lotus flower is unstained by water, so Nirvana is unstained by sins. As water cools feverish heat and quenches thirst, so Nirvana cools passions and removes cravings.'

(From the *Questions of King Malinda*)

➤ Some modern texts that show the importance and power of writing

Rebirth and Karma

'As a goldsmith, taking a piece of gold, reduces it to another newer and more beautiful form, just so this soul, striking down this body … makes for itself another more beautiful form … Truly this soul is Brahman … According as one acts, according as one conducts himself, so does he become. The doer of good becomes good; the doer of evil becomes evil.'

(From the *Brahadaranyaka Upanishad*)

Extract on Humanism

'Brief and powerless is Man's life; on him and all his race the slow, sure doom falls, pitiless and dark. Blind to good and evil … matter rolls on its relentless way. For Man, condemned … to pass through the gate of darkness, it remains to worship at the **shrine** his own hands have built.'

(Bertrand Russell, 1909)

Guru Nanak's Japji

'There is one God, Eternal Truth is His Name; maker of all things, fearing nothing and at enmity with nothing. Timeless is His image … If a man sings of God and hears of Him And lets love of God sprout within him, All sorrow shall depart.'

(From the *Guru Granth Sahib*)

Story of the Creation

'In the beginning God created the heavens and the earth. Now the earth was formless and empty … God said, "Let there be light," and there was light. God saw the light was good … God saw all that he had made, and it was very good.'

(From *Genesis* 1.1–5)

True Religion

'Righteousness does not consist in whether you face towards the East or the West. The righteous man is he who believes in God and the Last Day, in the angels and the Book and the prophets; who, though he loves it dearly, gives away his wealth to his kinsfolk, to orphans, to the destitute, to the traveller in need and to beggars, and for the redemption of captives … who attends his prayers.'

(From *Sura* 2:176–7, *Qur'an*)

The Lord's Prayer

'This, then, is how you should pray: "Our Father in heaven, hallowed be your name, your kingdom come, your will be done on earth as it is in heaven. Give us today our daily bread. Forgive us our debts, as we also have forgiven our debtors. And lead us not into temptation but deliver us from the evil one."'

(Jesus in *Matthew* 6:9–14)

ACTIVITY TWO ••

1. The following phrases have been taken from the extracts you read in Activity One. They are examples of some of the aspects of religion that you have been learning about throughout this book. Match each phrase with one of the aspects of religion provided.

Aspects of religion	Example
Belief	To give of one's wealth to family, orphans, needy, travellers, beggars
Stories	Pray then like this
Ethics	So Nirvana cools passions and removes cravings
Rituals	In the beginning God created the heavens
Experiences	There is but one God

2. Find your own examples from the extracts for two of the aspects shown.

NOW TRY THIS •••••••••••

Explain in your own words what one text tells you about the religion it comes from.

ACTIVITY THREE ••••••••••••

Do you have a favourite piece of writing, like a poem, a short story or a song lyric? If so, write down what it is and why you like it. If not, which of the extracts on the previous page do you like the most? Write down why you like it.

KEY WORDS

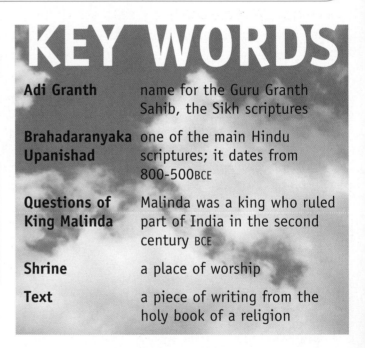

Adi Granth	name for the Guru Granth Sahib, the Sikh scriptures
Brahadaranyaka Upanishad	one of the main Hindu scriptures; it dates from 800-500BCE
Questions of King Malinda	Malinda was a king who ruled part of India in the second century BCE
Shrine	a place of worship
Text	a piece of writing from the holy book of a religion

6. So what does it mean to be religious? A debate.

SKILLS

- **thinking about** what you have learned,
- **finding out** and reflecting on what you found easy and hard to learn,
- **summarising** what you think is most important and why,
- **talking about** what you have learned,
- **deciding on** what you think about aspects of religion,
- **expressing** your ideas about what it means to be religious

We have looked at what religion is about, and where it came from. We have also learned why some people are religious and in what different ways. This unit brings your previous work together through a class debate.

A debate means arguing for or against an idea (called the **motion**) and taking a vote on it at the end. To do this, someone has to put forward the motion (the **proposer**), and someone else has to oppose it (the **opposer**). The proposer and the opposer each make a speech to convince the audience that their view is right. Two other people support the proposer and the opposer with a smaller speech each. When these four people have spoken, the **chair person** invites anybody else to speak for or against the motion, usually in turn, (called 'opening it up to the **floor**') until everybody has had their say, or time runs out. The proposer and opposer then briefly sum up the arguments for their views, and the chair person asks all present to vote for or against the idea. In a debate, the idea is usually set out by the chair person in the following way: 'This **house** believes that …'. The proposer is then asked to begin the debate.

▶ A debate taking place in the House of Commons. Notice how the room is laid out. Can you pick out the chair person?

Here is the motion for this debate:

'This house believes that being religious means that a person attends a place of worship regularly.'

ACTIVITY ONE ••

Now the motion is set out, you need to prepare your speech. If you are one of the four main speakers, your speech will need to be longer than if you are going to contribute from the floor. Here are some things to consider:

- Decide if you are in favour of the motion or not.
- If you are, think of all the reasons why you are in favour.
- If you are against the motion, think of all the reasons why you are against it.
- If you are not sure whether you agree with the motion or not, think about some reasons both for and against it.
- Make sure that you have some **evidence** for your reasons, such as facts or figures.
- Decide what your most important reasons and points are, and write these down first. Put less important ones afterwards.

Here is an outline of a speech:

'Ladies and gentlemen, …

I should like to support/oppose/change the motion.

My main reason is …

This is because …'.

NOW TRY THIS ....

Think about the arguments that people who disagree with you might use to support their view. Work out in advance how you might try to persuade others that their arguments are weak. Use this writing frame:

'You may hear that ... [insert an argument somebody might use against your point of view]. However, do not be persuaded by this. That argument is weak, because ... [insert your reason for disagreeing with the argument and your evidence why it is not convincing].'

ACTIVITY TWO ....

Take part in the debate and vote.

ACTIVITY THREE ....

When the debate is over ask yourself these questions:

- Did your view win or lose the debate?
- Why do you think this was?
- If you won, how did the other side take it? If you lost, how did you feel? Why?
- What do you think will happen next?

KEY WORDS

Chair person	the person who runs the debate by calling on people to speak in turn, organises the vote at the end, and whose decision is final
Evidence	reasons or facts to support a point of view
Floor	the ordinary people taking part in the debate
House	the group or class having the debate
Motion	an idea or statement that is to be debated and voted on
Opposer	the person who disagrees with the idea and opposes it
Proposer	the person who puts the idea forward and supports it

SUMMARY OF UNIT 6

Lesson 2

You have learned how to develop and use case studies to find out what being religious means for particular people.

Lesson 3

You have learned how to present your findings from an investigation into what being religious means, using PowerPoint.

Lesson 1

You have learned how to carry out an investigation into what being religious means for some religious people.

So what does being religious mean?

Lesson 4

You have learned how being religious means similar and different things for some key figures in religion by imagining that they were your guests at a dinner party.

Lesson 6

You have learned how to debate what being religious means and come to a class decision on what it means.

Lesson 5

You have learned what being religious means by looking in-depth at some religious texts, and learning how to interpret

Glossary

Adi Granth   name for the Guru Granth Sahib, the Sikh scriptures

Agnostic   someone who doubts the existence of a god or gods

Akhirah   Muslim belief in the Day of Judgement

Amrit   a liquid of water and nectar used by Sikhs to initiate new members of the Khalsa

Anti-Semitism   hostility to or prejudice against Jews

Atheist   someone who does not believe in a god or gods

Brahadaranyaka Upanishad   one of the main Hindu scriptures; it dates from 800-500BCE

Brahman   the one eternal reality or power for Hindus that is in everyone and everything

Buddha   the 'enlightened' or awakened one; the name given to Siddhartha Gautama

Chalice   a large cup or goblet used for the wine during the Mass

Christ   the Greek word for 'Messiah'; a title for Jesus used by Christians

Church   a place of worship for Christians. Other places might include a chapel or cathedral

Covenant   a promise or agreement; also known as a 'testament'

Creed   a statement of beliefs (from the Latin 'credo' meaning 'I believe')

Crucifix   a cross with the figure of the suffering Jesus on it

Crusade   a strong campaign against a person, group or practice that you think is mistaken

Denomination   the tradition or teachings followed in a place of worship

Dharma   teachings of the Buddha

Disciple   a learner or follower, usually of Jesus

Dukkha   suffering and everything unsatisfactory

Enlightenment   the Buddhist term for realising the truth about life

Faith   complete trust or confidence

Genesis   first Book of the Jewish Torah and the Christian Bible

God   the power, reality, cause or explanation for or behind everything

Gospel   a word that means 'good news'. Some books in the New Testament are called gospels

Guru   Sikh and Hindu term for religious teacher

Heaven   where God is found to his full extent

Hell   where God is absent; separated from God

Holy Spirit   Christian term for God's activity in the present

Id ul Fitr   Muslim festival marking the end of Ramadan, the month of fasting

Inter-religious   discussion and activities that go across religions to try to produce greater understanding

Jibril   one of the angels of God who brought messages to Muhammad; known as Gabriel to Jews and Christians

Karma   Hindu and Buddhist principle that determines the consequences of one life for another

Kippah   a head covering worn by Jewish men and boys, sometimes or all the time

Kosher   food that Jews are allowed to eat

Krishna   one of the most popular of the Hindu gods who came to earth in human form

Mandir   a place of worship and community activity in Hinduism

Mass   a service where worshippers remember the sacrifice of Jesus on the cross through receiving bread and wine. The bread represents Jesus' body and the wine represents his blood. In some churches this service is called Eucharist or Holy Communion

Messiah   a Hebrew word meaning 'anointed one'; the person the Jews expected to come to save them from their enemies

Moksha release from the cycle of being born and dying

Monotheism belief in one God

Nirvana he state of perfect peace, free from selfish desires

Oxfam a charity that serves the poor throughout the world by helping developing countries

Paten a special plate used to serve small round wafers of bread during the Mass

Patriarch the male head of a family; a biblical person regarded as a key ancestor of the Jewish people

Pentecost a festival that celebrates the giving of the Jewish Torah to Moses

Pesach the festival of Passover, which celebrates the rescue of the Jews' ancestors, the Israelites, from slavery in Egypt. It is held in Spring each year

Peter the leader of the first group of Jesus' disciples

Philosophical meaningful, understandable or logical

Precept an instruction or law

Prejudice an unfair opinion that is not based on reason or experience

Prophet for Jews and Christians, a spokesperson for God; prominent figure in the Old Testament/Jewish Bible who teaches the people God's message

Reincarnation a belief shared by Hindus, Buddhists and Sikhs that human beings are born into new lives in this world after they die

Ritual a ceremony or pattern of actions used in religious worship

Roman Catholic the community of Christians throughout the world whose spiritual leader is the Pope in Rome

SACRE a group of people who have responsibility for religious education in each local area in England and Wales (Standing Advisory Council for Religious Education)

Sacrifice an act of killing an animal or person as an offering to a god

Sangha the brotherhood of Buddhist monks

Sanskrit the ancient sacred language of the Hindu scriptures

Scripture a piece of writing, a text or a book regarded as very special or sacred

Sermon a talk given to worshippers on a religious topic by a leader

Shaman a person regarded as having access to the world of good and evil spirits, especially among some peoples of Asia and America

Shrine a place of worship

Shruti 'that which is heard'; a term applied to the four Vedas, including the Upanishads

Smriti 'that which is remembered'; a term applied to some Hindu scriptures

Soul the spiritual part of a human being, often regarded as the part of them that never dies, that is, immortal

Supernatural something beyond the ordinary, scientific, natural understanding or explanation of things

Superstition a widely held belief in supernatural powers bringing good or bad luck

Synagogue the Jewish place of worship

Temple a place of worship for Buddhists, although the word is also used for other religious buildings

Torah the most sacred book of Judaism, consisting of five smaller books containing the law, teaching and guidance of God; it was given to Moses on Mount Sinai, and is now kept in the Ark (cupboard) of a synagogue

Totem a natural object or animal believed by a group of people to have spiritual power and adopted by them as an emblem. A totem pole is a pillar on which totems are hung or carved

Ultimate questions important questions concerning what we believe about life

Upanishads word meaning 'to sit down near'; groups of teachings added to the Vedas at a later date

Vedas word meaning 'knowledge'; applied to the four oldest scriptures

Virgin Mary Jesus' mother

Vishnu Hindu God – the preserver

Index